Born to Dig

A Gardener's Chronicle

Born to Dig

A Gardener's Chronicle

A memoir

David L Haigh

Matador
9 Priory Business Park,
Wistow Road, Kibworth Beauchamp,
Leicestershire. LE8 0RX
Tel: 0116 279 2299
Email: books@troubador.co.uk
Web: www.troubador.co.uk/matador
Twitter: @matadorbooks

ISBN 978 1800461 727

British Library Cataloguing in Publication Data.
A catalogue record for this book is available from the British Library.

Printed and bound in Great Britain by 4edge Limited
Typeset in 11pt Minion Pro by Troubador Publishing Ltd, Leicester, UK

Matador is an imprint of Troubador Publishing Ltd

To Peggle

Contents

Foreword

David is a determined man. He refers to this trait as his "stubborn streak", but whatever we call this kind of temperament, I think it probably serves a gardener well. You need to be persistent if you're going to grow things, not to be defeated by the lack of control that is a gardener's lot. Pests, weather, disease; your crop may be ravaged by all or none, with dizzying unpredictability.

There is something of the same quality in David's writing: his style is solid and down-to-earth. As you read, you trust him. He is the kind of man, appropriately enough, to call a spade a spade.

David was a member of my writing workshop for two years. What I particularly appreciated about him was his willingness to have a go at whatever arcane text or writing exercise I suggested. He read poetry and postmodernist prose, researched poetic rhythm, and considered the ethics of biography; whatever I requested of the group, David would always do the work. He was often bemused by what he found, but always kept an open mind, and was refreshingly honest about his reactions.

This is a marvellously readable, informative and entertaining account of a life. From his early success growing cabbages as a young lad in the garden of his parents' first home of their own, it is clear that he loves growing things. We follow him as he embarks on a bold journey, leaving his Cumbrian village to drive six hours to agricultural college in Essex, then Kew Gardens in London, and eventually to Africa!

I loved reading about his rural childhood: playing football with an inflated rubber bladder and cumbersome boots; piling into one of the few village houses that had a TV; collecting rosehips for 4d a pound; selling fresh-picked mushrooms to Geordies on their way to Blackpool; turning up his nose at the local delicacy, "potted meat", which he describes temptingly as *small bits of bone held together in a greasy wobbly mass*. I like to imagine Grandad Longstaff taking his bar of carbolic soap to the river for his annual bath. David has affectionate memories of the many people with whom he studied and worked, and he includes some good anecdotes. I love his account of turning on the irrigation in Kew's Palm House at the end of a long shift, when one desultory family refuses to depart promptly at closing time! The sheer scale of the gardens becomes apparent on reading that he and another student spent five solid weeks raking leaves.

David's time in Lesotho, employed by the Overseas Development Agency, is fascinating to read about. It is bizarre to imagine him in his Vauxhall Cavalier, teaching tractor-driving in an arid, mountainous landscape ill-suited to either vehicle! I am grateful to him for introducing me to the charity Solar Aid, which provides solar lamps to the locals, thus helping them avoid the pollution and eye disorders caused by kerosene.

In keeping with his personality, the emphasis throughout is on practicality. Yet David's emotional honesty is moving. He describes his discomfort as a young man, feeling trapped by his mother's religious expectations. Many years later, upon the birth of his first child, he asks naively, 'Why has she got a pointed head?' This willingness to laugh at himself is coupled with an even more impressive willingness to look back on his own behaviour and wish he had acted differently; for example, when he refers to *my own hard-done-by sorrow* at the end of his first marriage. It seems fitting, then, that the book ends with his conversion to the no-dig method of vegetable growing; after a lifetime of digging, David is still curious and open enough to try a radically different method – and share its success with us too.

Dr Vicki Bertram

Preface

The seeds of my life story were sown in the early part of this century. It all began one winter's evening whilst the red wine was flowing freely. As was often the case, I was relating a story from my childhood to Barbara, my partner. My enthralled (maybe just tolerant) listener persuaded me to commit to paper the saga of our fearless neighbour. Mr Proctor had killed a large rat as it raced around our living room on a hot summer's evening. Over the next few years, a few other tales were added to that of Claude and the Rat. They stayed in a filing cabinet until 2016.

Writing my life story wasn't considered an option. A few short stories don't make a book was my take on it. Besides, I was quite happy with my part-time jobs of writing gardening articles, running practical gardening courses and hosting garden holidays.

After finally retiring in 2015, I soon felt the need for a new challenge and some mental stimulation. Barbara suggested I write my memoir. I didn't feel confident enough to embark on such a daunting undertaking.

I felt I needed a jolt of inspiration – something to kick-start my brain into new ways of thinking – something to improve my writing and take it down fresh avenues.

It was by pure chance that I came across a flyer for a writing course in the Kirkby Stephen Bookshop. The venue for the course was 50 miles from our home in Carlisle. The final 2 miles were down a narrow farm track to an isolated farmhouse, high in the fells above Kirkby Stephen, close to the Settle to Carlisle railway line. The journey was a step back to the future. Revisiting the land of my early years reignited many of the experiences from my first two decades.

My reminiscences would have to be written in a way which, to the reader, would come over as more vibrant and engaging than anything I had produced to date. Any success I have achieved in this endeavour owes a great deal to the skills and tutoring abilities of Vicki Bertram, the course leader. She taught me aspects of writing I didn't know existed and even got me writing poetry on at least three occasions. Her workshops put heavy demands on the brain cells, but were always most enjoyable. All course members were supportive of each others' work and always gave constructive criticism. Most importantly, the workshops were fun.

During the time we attended Vicki's course, my memoirs went from the age of twenty to seventy. Three score years and ten seemed a good point at which to stop. And so it would have been were it not for an unexpected development in the spring of 2019. The itch to move house to a different area had been scratched on a few previous occasions. For varying reasons, we had stayed put in Cumbria. But the itch kept erupting, until in March 2019, we knew we had found the cure in Castle Douglas, Kirkcudbrightshire. The period of moving, all that it entailed and the creation of a new garden with my conversion to no-dig gardening just had to be recorded in this my gardener's chronicle.

Acknowledgements

The fact that these memoirs have been written is down to my wife, Barbara. She first suggested the idea and has chivvied me along to get the job done. During this time, she has patiently read and reread sections of the manuscript whilst correcting my spelling, grammar and punctuation. The artworks on the cover and inside the book are examples of her taste and drawing skills.

Had it not been for the guidance and cajoling of the late Henry Noblett (former Head of Horticulture at Newton Rigg College) and Border Television's gardening guru, my life would have been very different.

I am extremely grateful to the Furrows Green Writers' Group. Vicki Bertram was an inspirational tutor who took all members of the group to new writing highs. My thanks are also due to the other group members, including Clare

Hallam, Sarah Kirkup, Karen Babayan, Dick Capel, Helen Murray, Janet Price, Sue Haywood and my wife Barbara for all the helpful hints and suggestions.

Finally, I wish to thank my son-in-law Ben Roberts for designing the book cover, and both Ben and Laura Roberts for advice and assistance with the book marketing.

One

How and Where it All Began for Me

It was the coldest winter for three centuries. The coldest ever recorded. Mother often told us how the snow came up to the top of the dykes (the Westmorland word for hedges) and stayed there for months on end.

I really shouldn't have been born. My mother had already produced a boy and a girl. But tragically my parents' first attempt at a third child was stillborn. So they tried again. With very little heating, the exercise involved in trying for another baby must have helped to keep my parents warm. But this activity only happened at the weekends. My father worked on the Settle to Carlisle railway. His working week was spent on Ribblehead viaduct. The journey to work by cycle took too long on a daily basis, so he came home on Friday evening and left very early on Monday morning.

Perhaps it was the dread of another cold winter, but I was determined to stay in the warmth of my mother's womb. This may well have been my parents' first experience of my stubborn streak. Anyway, I managed to keep it up for four weeks after my due date. I eventually arrived just before midnight on 23rd December 1947. I weighed a hefty 10 pounds. It must have been the most strenuous ordeal imaginable for my tiny mother, who gave birth to me at my grandparents' house, known as Inglenook in the small Westmorland village of Soulby.

Mam and Dad didn't know what to call me until the arrival of the village carol singers. *Once in Royal David's City* was belted out by the Soulby gospel singers, and the naming question was solved.

My parents rented Lilac Cottage, about 300 yards away on the southern side of the Scandal Beck – a small river which runs through the centre of the village. After the death of my grandparents, we moved to Inglenook. It was my mother's inheritance and her share of her parents' will. Inglenook was valued at £1,000 at that time. After my father's death in 1986, the house was sold for £42,000. In 2020, it was valued at £210,000.

My first significant memories go back to 1953. It was the Queen's Coronation and, like the rest of the country, our village joined in the celebrations. However, for me it was not a joyous time, rather an occasion which left me with bitter memories for years to come. Soulby decided that a carnival with everyone dressed up, particularly as someone important, would be the best way to commemorate this Royal extravaganza. It seems the village was in the vanguard of this current obsession with celebrity status. Anyway, my mother decided I should go as Princess Anne. The reason for this absurd choice was due to my blond, curly locks. Mother was very proud of them. I hated them; what made it even more unbearable was that she insisted that my hair was left to grow long. It was embarrassing enough to have hair like a girl, let alone be dressed up in a

Young David – 1952

costume as one, especially a princess. Despite repeated displays of beetroot-red faced screeching and foot-stamping, no amount of tantrums would get me out of this life-scarring role.

Ironically, when long hair for young men became trendy in the era of hippies and flower power, my hair decided to beat a hasty retreat to the back of my head. In a desperate attempt to retain what as a child I detested, I resorted to the Bobby Charlton-style comb over, which I held down with glue-like hairspray. My crowning glory resembled Shredded Wheat.

***

Lilac Cottage

Lilac Cottage was home for the first eleven years of my life. Back then, we belonged to Westmorland, one of the counties removed at a stroke by government in the early 1970s. I still regret the demise of Westmorland; it feels as if part of my heritage was removed by insensitive bureaucrats.

Built in the 1700s, this pokey, white-washed, two-up two-down housed me, my brother, John, mother, father and elder sister, Joyce. My parents rented the cottage from Frank Walton, a local Methodist preacher. He had so many business interests he virtually ran the village single-handed. Frank was the village carpenter and chimney sweep. He sold petrol, ran the taxi firm and charged large glass batteries which powered the wirelesses (radios).

The house had a leaky roof, no toilet and no bathroom. When it rained, tin buckets collected the water pouring in from the sky. The intervals between the plops as the water hit the buckets told us how heavily it was raining. Looking back now, I can't for the life of me think why my father didn't insist on old Frank repairing the roof. I guess his answer would have been – 'We don't pay much rent and its best not to cause any ill-feeling in case he puts up the rent, or worse still, evicts us.' The poorer members of society knew their place back in the 1950s; tenants' rights didn't amount to much.

Ceramic chamber pots decorated with red roses were kept under every bed. For many years, my brother and I shared the same bed and the same pot. During really cold spells, my mam (mother) always told us tales from her childhood. 'It was so cold the chamber pot froze. Things were far worse in my youth. You don't know you're born. Stop moaning.' Sadly, we didn't see it like that and took no comfort from her sorry plight.

In those early years, we had an earth closet. It was about 100 yards away, in our vegetable garden, near the primary school. Nobody relished the idea of going to the lavatory on a freezing or wet and windy winter's night. When needs must it was a case of taking a torch or an oil lamp, running down the hill, sitting on the cold wooden seat and performing the necessary bodily functions. Hard Izal toilet paper was too expensive, so back copies of the

Cumberland and Westmorland Herald found a second use. We were recycling paper long before it became environmentally friendly. Maurice Birkbeck, our near neighbour and farmer, would collect the end product once a year with his tractor and trailer, and then spread it on the land. My, did it stink, but I guess it was more natural and organic than flushing it down the toilet and sending it on its way to a sewage treatment works and out to sea.

***

Lilac Cottage was joined on two sides by larger houses. At the back lived Nellie Walton, sister of Frank, and on one side Claude and Annie Proctor were our neighbours. Now Auntie Nellie (she wasn't our auntie really) had a fear of mice. Mam always got the job of setting her traps and dealing with the dead ones. At the top of our stairs was a small walk-in cupboard backing onto Nellie's house. The back of the cupboard was made of thin plywood. Mam and Nellie would have regular chats through this wall. It was a bit like a telephone kiosk without the need for a phone. I still recall the hollow, echoing sound of Auntie Nellie tapping on the plywood and mother going upstairs and into the cupboard.

The conversation would go something like this – 'Myra, I've caught a mouse. Can you come around?'

To which Mam would reply without fail – 'Yes, I'll be there in a minute.'

When you opened the front door of the cottage, the stairs were directly in front of you. The door on the left led into the scullery and the one on the right into the living room.

Mice were often to be seen in our living room. They would scurry and squeak around the crate of the range. The range was a big, black, cast-iron beast, which had a dominant, brooding presence. It housed the fire, a boiler to heat water and the oven. Mother used to blacklead the range with enough elbow grease to make it sparkle.

There was a swinging crane for hanging jam pans and a wooden clothes dryer, which could be raised and lowered over the fire. Wednesday was baking day. During hot summer days, the heat from the crackling and spitting logs being burned to keep the oven at the correct temperature caused beads of sweat to run down Mam's face. She baked scones, gingerbread, fruit loaves and rock buns. The house smelt like a bakery, and the end products tasted even better. My abiding memory of the range is the divine smell and texture of bread toasted on a three-pronged toasting fork. Electric toasters have never matched up. Cheese toasted on the fire spluttered as it dripped onto the coals. The taste was far superior to that toasted under a modern grill.

Washdays were every Monday. All the windows would steam up and the whole house had a damp feel to it. The scullery was similar to every other in a working-class house of the 1950s. In one corner there was a built-in "copper" (large boiler) for heating the water, a "dolly tub" (wooden tub) where the clothes were washed with the aid of a "posser" (wooden tool) to move them around and a wrought iron "mangle" with two rollers through which the clothes had the excess water squeezed out. Turning the handle to rotate the rollers required considerable strength. The housewife of that era certainly worked extremely hard for six days a week. The Sabbath must have been a godsend.

At the front of Lilac Cottage there was the coal shed, a rickety old tin-clad construction; a cobbled yard with two narrow borders next to the cottage and at the front one white lilac tree and one mauve, one either side of the front gate. Apart from the coal shed, this was my mother's domain. She was responsible for the frontage. The doorstep was cleaned regularly, weeds between the cobbles removed with an old knife as soon as they saw the light of day, and each summer a spectacular display of alternating blue lobelia and white alyssum greeted visitors and passers-by.

My love of gardening and fascination with the world of plants can be traced back to 1955, to the age of eight. The reason I can be so sure of the accuracy of my memory is down to the introduction of a particular plant fertilizer called "Plantoids" – plant growth tablets. These were championed by none other than Fred Streeter, a BBC gardening guru in the mid-1950s. When Plantoids hit the shops, great claims were made for their beneficial effects. Mam just had to have some. She was not alone. One tablet was put in each planting hole. Disappointingly, there was no difference in the plants' performance whatsoever from previous years. When the plants were removed after summer was over, the tablets were still intact. So if they hadn't dissolved, they hadn't released any plant food.

Although this was very disappointing, it actually sparked my curiosity into the growth of plants.

My brother John and I had great fun playing on the wall next to the lilac trees. We would sit on the flat-topped wall and, using the tree branches as pretend levers, imagine ourselves as train or lorry drivers. The trees didn't seem to take any harm as no branches were broken intentionally by our harmless games. In fact, any pruning which occurred was probably responsible for them flowering profusely every year. That was until my dad thought he would make life easier for my overworked mam and relieve her of all the back-breaking weeding by applying sodium chlorate to the cobbles. The weeds certainly bit the dust. Unfortunately for the lilac trees, and more especially my poor dad, the trees were almost killed outright by this potent weed killer. They never regained their full health, and Dad, who wasn't blessed with green fingers, had to live with Mam's wrath and constant reminders of his near fatal mistake for years to come.

***

It was a warm summer's evening in 1956. My brother John and I were sitting on our weary, two-seater sofa. Mam was darning socks in front of the range. It was Wednesday – baking day. The residual warmth from the coal and logs which had heated the oven was stifling, even with the front door open. The smoky aroma of scones, rock cakes and gingerbread lingered throughout the cottage.

We were listening to the wireless. Regular adjustments to the large dial were needed to keep the crackling radio on station. Only three homes in the village had a television. With only one channel and a few hours of broadcasting a day, they would probably have been watching David Attenborough searching for a Komodo dragon in Borneo. *Zoo Quest* was the first wildlife documentary series on television. That evening, we experienced live wildlife in our living room.

The tranquil domestic bliss was suddenly interrupted by hysterical screaming from Mam. John and I leapt to our feet.

'What's the matter, Mam?' asked John.

'A rat! There's a rat in here!'

In unison, we all jumped onto the furniture and looked at each other, panic-stricken. Our expressions showed beyond any shadow of a doubt that we were scared witless. That was before John and I had seen the gruesome beast.

We were used to mice; after all, we shared our humble home with them. Mother wasn't at all frightened of them. Although John and I were a little scared, we could control our fear. Rats were a different proposition entirely and we were all petrified. So we had a dilemma as to what we were going to do about this rodent invader. We couldn't stand on the furniture all night and none of us dared go hunting it. Even if we tried to trap it, we knew that cornered rats go for the throat of a human. Hearsay or not, we daren't risk it.

This was where Claude Proctor came to the rescue. With the rat hiding, or resting behind the furniture, Mam ran out of the house in her highly charged emotional state and rattled the door knocker of our nearest neighbours, Claude and Annie Proctor.

'Whatever's the matter, Myra? You look as if you've seen a ghost.'

'A rat, there's a rat in our living room, Mr Proctor.'

A retired bank manager from County Durham, Mr Proctor was in his mid-sixties. A Captain Mainwaring figure, the rather pompous but kind-hearted old boy was an excellent neighbour. Standing around 5 ft 8 ins tall, he was heavily set with a forward-facing waistline. His shoulders and head were starting to slope forward. He took great pride in his appearance and was always dressed in polished black shoes, a dark suit and grey waistcoat, complete with pocket watch on a silver chain.

Claude was a brilliant if boastful gardener. He enthralled me with tales of his gardening prowess. According to him, he grew gooseberries the size of hens' eggs. Potatoes as big as his forearm. Leeks the length of his fork handle. Even as a small boy, I realised Mr Proctor was prone to exaggeration, but he did tell some captivating stories. This time, however, there was no doubting his bravery.

Armed with a heavy stick, he entered Lilac Cottage shouting – 'Don't worry, Myra. I'll get the bounder.'

Still standing on the furniture and shaking with fear, we watched as Claude flushed out the unwanted visitor. Then John and I saw what Mam had seen earlier – a gigantic, dark brown rat. It raced around the room in circles. It's hard to say who was the more frightened, the rat or us. Claude raised the stick and began lashing out, but the rat was too fast and it sped round squealing. There was no escape from the big white hunter. Eventually, it tired. Claude moved in for the kill and struck it with a mighty blow. The rat jerked once, twice. It still wasn't dead. Three or four more furious thwacks rendered it motionless.

A smile began to break out across the victor's face as he uttered the words – 'That's got the devil.'

He scooped it up on the fire shovel and took it outside. What he did with it then we didn't know and didn't care. Mam thanked Mr Proctor profusely.

'All in a day's work, Myra,' replied the old fellow, pushing out his chest with pride. What a hero he turned out to be. Never again would we doubt his claims to greatness.

I daresay when he told the story of the day he killed the neighbours' rat, the animal would have been the size of a colossal cat with 2-inch long, fanged teeth. Still, we thought Claude would have been entitled to elaborate his hunter's tale. His heroic efforts were never forgotten at Lilac Cottage.

The rat was real enough. However, there were some uncanny happenings at Lilac Cottage which denied explanation.

**

The early evening of 11th February 1953 was bitterly cold. My brother, John, my mother and I were sitting huddled around the coal fire. At 6.30 pm, we heard three loud knocks on the front door. Rat, tat, tat went the echoing sound of the large iron door knocker.

'Who can that be?' Mother muttered somewhat crossly as she went to the door. When she opened the door, there was no one to be seen. This did nothing to improve her demeanour. 'It must have been children playing games,' she complained, 'they want their backsides spanking.' As knock and run was a prank we all played, John and I felt sure Mother was correct in her assumption and thought it best to nod sagely whilst concealing the smirks which were bubbling under our faces.

Next day, however, we discovered that our Auntie Ida (who incidentally was our great-auntie, Ida May Henderson) had passed away at precisely 6.30 pm the previous night. That was the exact time of the rat, tat, tat on our door. I don't remember anything else about Auntie Ida. I was only five years old when she died but have never forgotten that haunting, metallic rattle of the door knob the moment she died.

It may have been a childish prank or more likely a paranormal event. As recent research has led me to discover that an earlier relative of Auntie Ida, called George Henderson, was the village blacksmith in Soulby and Crosby Garrett, then maybe, just maybe, he made our door knocker. With supernatural powers from beyond the grave, he was able by way of the rat, tat, tat to tell us of Auntie Ida's passing.

Three years later, my sister, Joyce, who had left home for the big metropolis of Penrith (population about 12,000), was home for the weekend. At the time, Lilac Cottage was undergoing a major transformation. In truth, our landlord was building a small lean-to extension to house a water closet and a sink. This was for us to be a massive leap into the twentieth century, as until now we had to walk a hundred yards to our garden to use the earth closet.

Whilst the work was going on, the doorway between the sitting room and the new build was covered with a sheet. Joyce was sleeping on the sofa in the sitting room. In the early hours, we were awoken by her terrified screaming. We ran downstairs to find her sitting bolt upright on the sofa, shaking uncontrollably with fear. When she finally became a little calmer, she told us a ghost had walked close by her and slipped out through the doorway into the night.

She always maintained it was a ghost, but it could just as easily have been one of the many tramps who passed regularly through the village in the late 1950s. Poltergeist or human, it scared my sister half to death, and the rest of the family found it difficult to sleep for some time after this apparition.

My own dalliance with anything approaching the paranormal wasn't in the least bit scary. As a boy of five or six, I would stand at the bedroom window and stare into the branches of the leafless trees. Figures like holograms would appear. They danced about from limb to limb. They weren't human. They weren't animal. More like a cross between the two. Happy, jumping visions which kept me transfixed as they played games such as tag and a kind of hopscotch.

Suddenly my trance would be broken. The trees were empty again. Where did these mystical creatures come from and where did they disappear to? I could only guess at their origins. Maybe they were cloud travellers. When the clouds were down at tree height that was when I could see their impish antics. They seemed to float on the wind from side to side and up and down. At irregular intervals, they would jerk about playing games. Were they all the same? No, there were many different forms, yet they all belonged to the group and all appeared happy together. What did they eat and drink? I thought they must get water from the clouds, but where did they get food and what did they eat?

If only I could get to the top of the trees I could see for myself. But I was too small to climb trees. I thought when I got older I would get into the treetops and wait for my imaginary friends to visit. Would they be friendly? Did they talk? I had so many questions to ask them.

Long before I was able to climb, my friends in the sky had vacated my world. I felt a big loss. But I had been the only one, as far as I knew, who had seen these creatures.

***

The early 1950s were days of miracles and wonder. Big square boxes produced moving pictures, and they spoke. These were the early days of television. The Birkbecks' living room at Castle Hill Farm was by far the most popular place for the village children to watch telly. The room was packed. Adults sat in chairs. We, the children, sat on the floor with our little legs crossed. Not a murmur came from our lips. The excitement mounted as the one-eyed monster flickered into life.

Fortunately for us it was only 20 yards from Lilac Cottage. The Bainbridges of Barney Scar also had a set, but the reception was much poorer. Their farmhouse was in a hollow, so Arthur (Barney) Bainbridge had a very tall aerial installed and a big magnifying glass put in front of the screen to improve reception. The improvement was negligible.

Watching at the Birkbecks' had more appeal. They had three children. Jean was the eldest, Harold was the same age as John, my brother, and Ian was my age. The Bainbridges had three girls. We were too young to like girls. In any case, the Birkbecks' floor was bigger so more of us could squeeze in. Mrs Birkbeck (Lillian) often treated us to squares. These were a kind of Westmorland delicacy, something like a square-shaped scone with a high lard content. The addition of butter and jam helped them slide down the throat easily.

Those early television sets suffered from problems of reliability. The cabinets were big in order to house the large tubes. However, the screens were pretty small – about 10 inches wide. Brands such as Pye and Echo were commonplace. The picture lacked definition. Although known as black and white sets, they were in fact shades of grey. Early televisions had buttons down the side of the screen. One was for *horizontal hold* and another for *vertical hold*. The picture often spun up and down or from side to side. The relevant knob had to be adjusted to rectify this fault. Frequently, the picture would take on the appearance of a snowstorm, or loads of jagged lines would cover the screen and a message would appear saying,

Interference is only temporary – please do not adjust your set. On many occasions, a thump with a fist on top of the box would sort out the problem.

Despite these glitches, our enjoyment was undimmed. We even watched the test card (a static picture) for some time whilst waiting for the programmes to start. One of my favourite programmes was *The Cabin in the Clearing.* This was a tale about white settlers who had made themselves a wooden home after clearing a space in the forest and driving out the Red Indians. The whites, who were portrayed as the heroes, defended themselves with guns against the Red Indians, who, armed with bows and arrows, were trying to regain their rightful territory. Other children's programmes at that time included *Billy Bunter, Flower Pot Men, Muffin the Mule* and *The WoodenTops.*

Football on television was a massive draw in the 1950s. Any fan from that time remembers the 1953 FA Cup Final between Blackpool and Bolton Wanderers, largely because of the performance of the legendary Stanley Matthews. For me, though, that doesn't hold the most vivid memories of football on the telly. That honour goes to Nana Thwaites, Mrs Birkbeck's mother. She was a fanatical supporter of Bishop Auckland, an amateur team from County Durham. Almost every year they played at Wembley in the FA Amateur Cup Final, and this was televised. Nana Thwaites got very animated, and whenever Bob Hardisty the Bishop Auckland captain got the ball, she would jump out of her seat and shout, 'Give it the works, Bob.' She brought the crowd into the living room.

***

Soulby hasn't had a primary school for decades. The buildings are still used as the village hall. I can remember a great deal about the layout of Soulby Primary School from the main door to the position of my desk and its inkwell. When I attended between the ages of five and eleven, the school was full, with about thirty pupils. There were two classes according to age. The school was divided into two rooms by a moveable partition. The larger section for the older children housed the solid fuel boiler. The cloakroom was built on at one end.

It was a bitterly cold place. During winter, the half-pint bottles of free milk often had about an inch of frozen milk on top. Blue tits that tried to get at the milk tore holes in the tin foil tops with their beaks. Toilets, which were outside, were very basic and smelly.

We had a fairly large playground which ran down to the Scandal beck. The beck was unfenced. Nowadays, that would be unthinkable. Health and Safety legislation would ensure that it was virtually impossible for us to learn to respect the dangers that are ever-present in the natural environment. Why didn't any child drown?

After school, the older boys came up with an invention for sailing up and down the river. It was to be a very basic raft. During its construction, I came to grief. In order for it to float, the raft was to have an empty 5-gallon oil drum on each corner. Planks of wood would then be tied on top with ropes to make a kind of platform for sitting on and paddling this aquatic craft. The smaller boys like me and George (Sonny) Brass were too little for any of this complex engineering. So we entertained ourselves by throwing the barrels to each other. All was fine until I failed to catch a flying barrel cleanly. The barrel spun round and one corner hit me on the forehead just above the eyes. The skin was punctured.

Blood started to ooze from the cut, slowly at first. I dabbed it with my hanky, which was probably pretty dirty. The rate of flow increased. With blood gushing out, I ran home as fast as my short, fat legs would carry me. Into Lilac cottage I rushed, crying more with fear than pain. Mam took one look at my head, sat me down, tried to calm me with kindness and called the doctor.

Doctor Byers came from Brough some 3 or 4 miles away. He sat me down in the scullery, put a kitchen towel over my head and inserted two or three stitches in the cut. The doctor praised me for my bravery and gave me two wine gums as a reward.

The big boys did finish the raft, but I never sailed on her. I am not sure there is any connection, but I have always preferred dry land. To this day, I can barely swim.

There was a small hill in the school playground used for sledging. Did it really snow every winter? I think most winters it did. When we weren't at school, we sledged in Maurice Birkbeck's field.

The farm was about 20 yards from Lilac Cottage. The sledging hill was much steeper and longer than the school hill – far more exciting. On one side there were ridges, somewhat like the moguls on a ski run. We called this part "bonkety bonk". Getting to the bottom without being thrown off was a major achievement which gained many boasting rites.

Playtime in and out of school was fun, and the happy memories remain. However, I don't remember learning anything useful at primary school. Being read Enid Blyton stories springs to mind and that's about it. Of the two teachers we had, the head teacher, Miss Harker (Lucy), must take the lion's share of the blame. Lucy was more interested in village gossip than inspiring pupils. Most days she would be heard criticising someone from the village. Whilst in full spate, Lucy would hog the boiler as she vigorously rubbed her hands together making loud ssshing noises. I secretly wished that one day the old witch would self-ignite.

One day, she made a particular vicious verbal attack on my Uncle James and the way he ran the village slaughterhouse. A cow had escaped as it was being taken on a rope to meet its death by the butcher wielding a humane killer. In a state of wild panic, the beast had run amok and crushed somebody's bicycle. Miss Harker had no qualms about relating this story to the other teacher, a Mrs Fothergill from Crosby Garrett, in full earshot of me and any children who cared to listen. If only she had put as much effort into teaching.

Mrs Fothergill was a good teacher. She was conscientious, kind and patient. Even so, she couldn't ignite my brain. Daydreaming was the only subject I excelled at. Often, my thoughts were infiltrated by pictures of my grandfather. I imagined him milking his cow, making hay or, best of all, sowing vegetable seeds.

How I wished I was helping him. Little wonder I failed the 11-plus. My failure to concentrate on schoolwork was a recurring theme all the way through until I left secondary school. The stimulus for change at the age of eighteen will become apparent later.

Two

Family and a Religious Upbringing

―――――――――――

My mother's side of the family was firmly rooted in Westmorland. Many of the children in this rural county were born and died on family farms. Upon leaving school, relatively few young people upped sticks. Farming was their inheritance. We didn't have a family farm. I didn't want to be a farmworker. I wanted to be a gardener. My mother led me to believe that my love of plants must have come from my father's father, Grandad Haigh. He had died long before I was born. Mam reckoned he had been a head gardener somewhere near Leeds. The gardening gene must have skipped a generation, was her theory. My dad never spoke of his dad. Mam said the memories were too painful for him. Apparently, Grandad Haigh had committed suicide by placing his head in a gas oven. Some years ago, my limited research found no evidence to prove either his job or cause of death. It seemed that the only Haigh that tied into my father's birthplace and age was a William Haigh, and he was recorded as a boot riveter in the 1911 census. I much preferred my mother's version of his occupation. She wouldn't have told me he was a head gardener if that wasn't the case.

Further research later revealed that Grandad Haigh had, by the time of his eldest son's wedding in 1924, changed his occupation to that of a gardener. Maybe he was too modest to claim the title of head gardener when he witnessed my uncle's wedding, or he may have risen to that position in later years. What I am sure about is Grandad Longstaff's close affinity with the land and his innate ability to grow crops. I feel both grandads deserve credit for my love of the soil and all the pleasure it has given me.

Grandad and Grandma Longstaff farmed at Smithfield in the hamlet of Little Musgrave. During this time, they raised two daughters and one son. Several years before I came along, my grandparents retired from full-time farming and moved a distance of about 1 mile to Inglenook in the village of Soulby.

My grandad, John Longstaff, had a short, sturdy, but not too stocky build. A lifetime of hard work was responsible for his near perfect physique. Being a tenant farmer was, so I was told, merely subsistence farming. My grandparents certainly didn't die rich.

Although he had retired from full-time farming, Grandad never lost touch with the land. Whilst at Smithfield, he started a butcher's business which had a slaughterhouse in Soulby and a shop in Kirkby Stephen. This business was handed over to his son James. Grandad had some old stone buildings, including a barn and a byre, in two small fields about 50 yards from Inglenook. Just outside the village he farmed two small fields know as Low Crossbars and High Crossbars, as well as a larger parcel of land called The Allotment near the neighbouring village of Crosby Garrett. A small stream ran through the centre of this field. It was in this tiny beck that Grandad had his annual bath. He did, however, wash daily in the kitchen sink and never smelt.

Bullocks were kept in the fields. Nearer home, he kept one milk cow. At milking time, Grandad sat on a three-legged stool, which he called a koppy, close to the cow's udders. His cap was turned back to front so as not to dig into the cow's stomach. This would have caused the cow to kick out and most likely knock the milk bucket over. When the cow occasionally got a bit uneasy, Grandad, who was a paragon of patience, would quietly utter the words 'cush, cush,' and serenity would be restored.

My grandad was a deeply religious man. For many years, he was a church warden. He never swore, or so I thought, until one day my illusion was shattered. Along with Sam, his able sheepdog, Grandad, with me at his side, was taking a small group of bullocks down the road to pastures new. One or two beasts broke loose and made a run for it. My angry grandad let rip with the words 'Oh bugger.' The shock of those words coming from my grandad's mouth hit me like a stone from a catapult.

Later that day, Mother said, 'David, you're very quiet. What's wrong?'

I told her, 'Grandad swore at the cattle.'

'Grandad would never, ever do that. You must have misheard.'

Looking back, it was hardly the sin of the century, but in my innocent childhood it became ingrained in my memory.

Similarly, the sight of Grandad making hay is as vivid today as it was in the mid-1950s. He pulled a very large, heavy wooden rake behind him as he turned the grass and moved it into rows to dry and become hay. He only had a small hayfield or surely he would have used horsepower.

Hedging, or dyking as it was called, meant laying a hawthorn hedge. This was the last job Grandad did. He got a thorn in his eye and came home feeling very tired and in bad fettle. A few days later, he passed away in his early seventies.

***

My grandmother Ada, Alice Longstaff, was a powerfully built farmer's wife who thrived on hard work. She had grey, tied-back hair. Most days, she wore a pinny. Grandma had a very imposing presence and was highly regarded as one of the elders of the village. She commanded great respect.

After the death of Grandad, Grandma kept one small field close to Inglenook. On this field were a barn, a stone-built lean-to which had been home to Sam, the long since deceased sheepdog, and a large rectangular wooden henhouse.

Grandma loved her hens. She kept about thirty, which consisted of one cockerel, some Rhode Island Reds, White Sussexes, White Leghorns – which were the least attractive breed but the best layers of that era – and one Wyandotte, which Grandma called Wingy. 1t laid very few eggs, but rather surprisingly for a hardened farmer for whom livestock had to earn its keep, she kept it as a pet.

John and I were taught the finer aspects of poultry husbandry by Grandma. We had to perform our chores on a daily basis before and after school. These involved regularly cleaning out the henhouse, feeding the birds and dealing with the broody ones. Broody hens just sit on eggs keeping them warm until they hatch. During this time they aren't laying. Every nest box contained a pot egg as a means of encouraging the hens to lay eggs in the nest boxes rather than anywhere else that might take their fancy. Hens that stayed on a nest for too long were broody. Grandma called these hens "clockers". She would lift them off the nest and confine them to a small wooden cage until they got over their maternal instinct.

The birds slept on perches above a raised wooden floor. Chicken manure built up on this floor and had to be scraped up and shovelled out. Hen fleas used to breed like crazy in the muck. These critters used to bite me with monotonous regularity every time I tackled this job. Grandma always told me that fleas only went for bad meat. I didn't find her remarks helpful or amusing, but didn't dare say anything which could have been taken as cheeky. Itchy skin just had to be suffered as an unpleasant side effect when mucking out the henhouse.

Biting fleas were nothing compared to the rats. John and I were frightened of the mice, which ate their way into the wooden feed bin known as a kist. Nearly every time the lid was lifted to get at the corn, several mice would race around the sides before escaping over the top rim. Mice held no fear for Grandma, nor the rats which occasionally found their way into the bins. My brother and I were terrified of rats, and when one was spotted, Grandma had to be called or the hens wouldn't have been fed. Unflinchingly, she would lift the kist lid with one hand then with a ladle in the other, she would delve into the food and bring out a scoopful of food. 'Don't be so daft,' she said to us, 'they are more frightened of you than you need be of them.'

The actual making of the hen food was the best job. It consisted of corn, Euveka, which was a kind of unadulterated corn flakes for hens, and Carswood spice, a bright red powder which gave the eggs a lovely deep orange colour. Potato peelings and any other vegetable leftovers were added with boiling water, and this concoction was mixed together in a bucket with a stick. Unlike more modern poultry food, "Crowdy", as it was called, didn't result in as many eggs being laid, but it smelt almost good enough to eat, especially on a frosty morning. The hens adored it. Cackling and pushing each other aside, their trough was emptied with great haste.

Collecting the eggs on a daily basis was a very pleasant job, which became even more so every Tuesday evening when we took the surplus eggs to Tim Pighill's house. Tim was an egg wholesaler who lived opposite Inglenook. The money we received was a great incentive which, along with a deeper understanding and affection for the birds, made keeping hens a most enjoyable and rewarding experience, despite the fleas and rats.

***

My father, Furniss Haigh, was born in Leeds on 18th November 1909. Furniss was his mother Elizabeth's maiden name. Dad came to Westmorland through his job as a plate layer on the Settle to Carlisle railway. In an earlier job, he had worked in a bakery. He blamed the heat in the bakery for losing his hair at an early age. Male pattern baldness due to inherited genes probably wasn't known about by the general population at that time.

The big perk of my dad's job was the free rail travel for himself and his family. This meant day trips to far-flung places like Carlisle. The station on the Settle to Carlisle line was built on a hill outside of Kirkby Stephen and known as Kirkby Stephen West. We made frequent visits to the marshalling yards and engine workshops in Carlisle. Although exciting, it was also a bit scary for me when we got, what seemed like, very close to some of the large noisy steam engines.

On one memorable occasion, I got my first brand-new bicycle from T.P. Bells of Carlisle. Their shop was near the cathedral and in fact the firm's name is still to be seen in large letters painted on the side of the building. The bike was a red Raleigh. When we got back to Kirkby Stephen I was full of nervous tension as I mounted my bike.

'Are you sure you'll be all right? Just go steady.'

'It'll be fine. Don't worry, Dad.'

Off I went down the town's back street at a reckless speed and totally out of control. Needless to say, panic soon set in, and after one almighty wobble I fell off and the bike came to a halt on an earth bank by the roadside. The only damage was to my pride and a few minor scratches to the knees.

Until Dr Beeching swung his axe in 1962/1963, Kirkby Stephen East Station was on the line from Darlington to Tebay and the Eden Valley. We often travelled on this line for part of the journey to my dad's relatives. Uncle Horace and his wife lived in a terraced house in the village of Glasshouses, near Pateley Bridge in the West Riding of Yorkshire. My only worthwhile memory from our visits was the wind-up His Master's Voice gramophone. After many turns of the handle, the contraption was fully wound. To begin with, the sound of the music came out quickly. Gradually, it slowed down until towards the end it sounded like a slurred drawl. It wasn't long before the music stopped. Despite these shortcomings, music coming out of a machine was a novelty for the Haighs.

On another occasion, we stayed at Green Farm, Ramsgill, near Pateley Bridge, with another of my dad's relatives called Norman Welleck. The final part of the journey involved a bone-shaking drive down a deeply rutted farm track in Norman's Land Rover. I recall being violently sick before we reached the farm. The property is part of Ramsgill Estate and is now a luxury self-catering farmhouse.

***

My dad was worse than useless at growing fruit and veg. He didn't have much affinity with the land or what grew where and why. Dad always set all his vegetables on Good Friday. It didn't matter if Easter was early or late. Cold or hot, wet or dry, everything was sown or planted on that one day. According to Father, that was the only spare time he had in spring, due to him working away from home from Monday to Friday. Shallots, rhubarb and broad beans were the only crops that produced anything worthwhile. I loved Good Fridays. With my little wooden wheelbarrow, I thought I was a great help.

Grandad Longstaff instinctively knew how and when to cultivate the ground. When to sow and when to plant was second nature to him. According to folklore, the old farmers would drop their trousers and put their bare bottoms on the soil in spring to gauge whether it was warm enough to sow their crops. I never saw Grandad do this. Maybe he did, but more likely he just knew by the feel of the soil and warmth of the air. His small vegetable plot at Inglenook grew the most splendid crops. In years to come, I would have the chance to take over Grandad's plot and his mantle as a grower of top-quality fruit and vegetables.

***

Myra Elizabeth Longstaff (Mam) was born on 2nd June 1911 just outside the village of Soulby at Smithfield, where her parents were tenant farmers. My mother was about 5 feet tall with a medium build. She had a round face, large brown twinkly eyes and hair which remained black without any artificial colourant well into her fifties. Mam was a confident, outgoing woman who played an active role in village life. She was a member of the Mothers' Union, and a firm believer in the Christian faith.

Our mam was a very determined lady with an uncrushable belief in God. She wanted her children to grow up with her values and to live by her code, which revolved around going to church and striving to be the best at whatever you chose to do. The going to church part ceased to be part of my life over fifty years ago, but I have always had a strong desire to achieve my goals. Mam firmly believed that anyone who fell from the straight and narrow must expect the dire consequences which would surely follow. She wanted what she regarded as the best for her children.

However, as I grew older I felt increasingly resentful at the way she exercised her control over me. She was constantly telling me to study hard, not to get involved with girls as they would jeopardise my career prospects and to keep well away from public houses. Many times I felt trapped and unable to be the person I longed to be. In time, I came to realise that this prison I lived in was down to my own personality. During my formative years between the ages of five to about fifteen, I had grown an introverted shell which I couldn't break out of. When I left home at the age of twenty, the cracks began to appear in my self-imposed restrictive armour.

***

My brother John was five years older than me. He was bigger, stronger and better at sports than me. We played a lot of Subbuteo (table football). John nearly always won. He delighted in winding me up every time I was in sight of the goal. 'He's in with a chance, but I'm afraid he'll waste it' was one of his most irritating lines. It was guaranteed to get me rattled and frequently miss easy chances. Big Brother usually came out on top when we played table tennis. I hated losing and he knew it. Taunting me was a source of great mirth for John.

We often went fishing for trout in the River Scandal. It was easier to catch fish after heavy summer rainfall when the beck was in flood. We dangled worms in the calmer water at the edge of the stream. If the float quickly disappeared under water, a jerk on the rod and more often than not a fish was hooked. Needless to say, I only hooked a few, but John usually got several.

When I was eleven, we moved to Inglenook. It wasn't long before we got our own television. Every Saturday afternoon, we watched the wrestling. In our fantasy world, we were the stars of the ring and imagined ourselves as our heroes, such as Mick McManus, Steve Logan and Jackie Pallo. The living room floor and settee was our ring. We knew all the holds and mimicked all the grunts and groans. Mam was not amused. 'It will end in tears,' she always said and usually that was true. The only one crying was me, not because I was hurt, but because I had been beaten as usual.

Although getting the better of me at home seemed to give him great pleasure, John always stood up for me when we played with the other boys in the village. If anyone tried to bully me, he came to my defence without fail. One of the most terrifying episodes was being dangled by one arm from the side of the bridge over the Scandal Beck by Michael (for some reason we called him Tom) Moffat. Tom was a tall, athletic boy about two years older than John, who had a boastful, bullying nature. This time, John told him he had gone too far and to hoist me back. Moffat pulled me back to safety whilst trying to laugh off his thoughtless and dangerous behaviour.

When I reached my early teens, I joined John working on a village farm (Barney Scar) at hay time. We loaded the bales of hay onto trailers in the fields and off again back at the barn next to the farmhouse. They had to be stacked in the barn. It was hard, sweaty work and hay seeds kept getting into your eyes. Hay time lasted about three weeks. The highlight of every day was the lavish farmhouse supper provided by Lizzie Bainbridge, the farmer's mother. At 9 pm, when work was over, we were fed lots of meat, salads and potatoes, washed down with mugs of hot tea. We got reasonably well paid and very fit from the strenuous physical work.

John took over the butcher's business in Kirkby Stephen founded by Grandad from our Uncle James in 1983. He retired in January 2009. Sadly, he died only a month later at the age of sixty-six. His wife Dorothy died in April that year.

***

My sister Joyce was ten years older than me. When I was a baby, she pushed me around in one of those massive prams with huge springs and large wheels. After primary school, she went to Kirkby Stephen Grammar School for girls. Joyce left school at sixteen with her matriculation. A qualification which meant she could train as a shorthand typist. This training took her to Penrith. It was there that she met her first husband, Cliff, the father of my three nieces Dawn, Gail and Karon. Joyce and Cliff married at St Luke's Church, Soulby on a snowy Easter Saturday.

Cliff got a job with ICI and they moved to the northeast. For a while, they lived in a flat in Saltburn. I visited one summer soon after Dawn was born. I have an old photo of me nervously holding this tiny baby.

Around about the same time, they had a black Burmese cat called Scamp. Scamp often ventured into neighbours' houses and went to sleep on any bed she could find. This didn't go down well with the neighbours, and to avoid any bad feeling, Scamp came to live with us. She was a very lithe feline and a good hunter. Scamp didn't have a long life compared to today's cats. Veterinary treatment of cats is much more effective now than then. But she was a much-adored family pet.

Joyce and Cliff moved to Guisborough. About thirty years ago, they got divorced. For twenty-eight years she was happily married to Jackie. Originally from Glasgow, Jackie lived in the northeast for many years but never lost his broad Glaswegian accent. Joyce died in February 2018, aged eighty. A year later, Jackie passed away at eighty-six years of age.

***

Like most children in the village, we were brought up in a God-fearing environment. Come to think of it, I can't recall any families who didn't believe in the Bible. Though ours was a Christian household, there was conflict.

My father came from the Methodist side of the divide. Mother's family were staunch Church of England. During my early years, the family attended Soulby Methodist Chapel, a Weslyan fortress close to the Black Bull Public House. The village pub was closed down in the mid-1950s. Why I mention this now will be revealed later. My theory as to why we were Methodists is, I think, because my mother felt she had to obey her husband's wishes, and this meant we all went to chapel. In later years, we changed our allegiance to St Luke's Church. This, I reckon, was down to my mother's stronger personality. I think Dad just gave in. He wasn't one for conflict. Dad preferred the path of least resistance and knew that sooner or later, Mam would get her way.

We attended; first, chapel, then in later years, church. Worshipping at least once a week without fail. Sunday school was also compulsory. I remember my time spent at chapel with greater clarity and even a small amount of pleasure. Chapel was much livelier than the stuffy C. of E. The preachers were all amateurs from various walks of life, including farmers, carpenters and shopkeepers. Most of their sermons were shorter and less boring than those delivered by the professional vicars at church. One chapel preacher I can see and hear now was a local farmer called Philip Wharton. He was a small grey-haired man with a chin that jutted out when he delivered his favourite one-liner – 'Ye are the salt of the earth.' He got this into every sermon at some point.

The chapel had regular social events, including the harvest festival sale. This took place a day or two after the service in the Sunday school room. The assembled throng would bid for tins, cakes and fresh produce. It was also the meeting point for The Band of Hope, an organisation for teetotal zealots. Several such worthy individuals were on the parish council. When the brewery applied for planning permission to improve the sanitation at the Black Bull, it was turned down. The upshot of this was the closure of Soulby's pub.

The family's defection to church occurred about the same time as we moved into Inglenook. St Luke's was just across the green from our new home. As well as being devoutly religious, Mam was a very talented musician. We had a piano in the sitting room, which she played daily. Hymns and classical music were her speciality. She was a member of the local choral society, something which I feel she thought elevated her social standing. Her attempts to teach me the piano fell on musically deaf ears and fat fingers which couldn't hit just one key at a time.

Playing *The Bonny Banks of Loch Lomond* was beyond my capabilities. Mam's prowess on the keyboards meant she was recruited by the vicar to play the church organ.

But her success wasn't enough. After a great deal of persuading, she managed to get my father involved in the upper echelons of church affairs. With mounting pressure from Mother and Bertie Meads, the vicar, he finally agreed to take on the role of church warden. Dad hated the limelight and the responsibility which went with this position. All he wanted to do in his spare time was read the newspapers, chop wood and fill in his football pools coupon. Maybe Bertie Meads couldn't find any other suspects for the post. I seem to remember he wasn't very well liked by his flock. They thought he was too aloof and felt he looked down on them with his one working eye (his other eye was made of glass). If he had spent more time drinking tea and gossiping, they would have said he was showing an interest in his parishioners.

He glided through the village, ghostlike, in a long, billowing cloak, beneath which his highly polished black shoes sparkled. My mother was probably his biggest fan and would hear no wrong of him. She spent a lot of time at the vicarage with Bertie and his wife, Bessie, presumably deciding on the hymns for forthcoming services. On one occasion, I had been doing some weeding and digging in the vicarage garden when Bessie called me in for tea and cakes. Mam and Bertie were at the far end of the large dining room table, discussing church music. Bessie went to the kitchen to collect the cakes. It was then that I noticed Bertie's arm under his cassock move around my mother's back. From that day forth, I always had niggling doubts about their relationship.

Way back then, the size of the church congregation was dwarfed by that of the chapel. This must have remained in a similar vein, because a few years ago, St Luke's closed its doors for the last time. The Methodist chapel is still welcoming worshippers. As for me, my church visits have for many years been limited to weddings, funerals and the occasional carol service. However, my religious upbringing has left a lasting impression on me. Even though I can't come up with any logical reasons to believe in and fear God, I will always feel guilty if I think or, worse still, say anything which could be taken as blasphemous.

Three

Village Life in 1950s Westmorland

W e just lived it. We didn't really appreciate it. Most days were spent outdoors from dawn to dusk. Children were allowed to roam and play wherever they wanted, both inside the village and the surrounding countryside. We even wandered as far as Crosby Garrett, the nearest village, about 1.5 miles away. Crosby was even smaller than Soulby, but on the plus side, the Settle to Carlisle railway line went through or rather over the far end of the village by way of a bridge. Trainspotting was very popular with lots of boys in that era.

Every time we left home, Mother would say, 'Be careful and don't speak to strangers.' In all honesty, not many strangers visited this rural county in the 1950s and '60s. Tramps were frequent visitors, a few of them returning regularly to beg for food and a few pennies. They often slept rough in farmers' barns. Young lads can be cruel and we would call them names like *stinker* and tease them mercilessly, always making sure they couldn't catch us. One fearsome-looking character wore a thick overcoat whatever the weather and sported a long, dense, bluish-grey beard. Not surprisingly, we called him Bluebeard. He would swear at us and wave his stick as he threatened revenge for the way we tormented him. One day, he came to the house begging, and as he walked past the window, he saw me and my brother in the living room. We knew he recognised us and immediately darted under the table in a terrified state. We daren't come out for what seemed like hours, until we were sure the coast was clear.

Bill and Annie Smith were down-and-outs who lived in the nearby village of Winton. He was tall and angular with broad shoulders and she was small and shrew-like. We never knew what their home was like but always imagined it was nothing more than a very basic shelter (probably part of a farm building). Every Tuesday, they would walk from Winton to Soulby refuse tip, on the outskirts of the village, not far from Crosby Garrett. The tip was a massive rodent-infested hole in the ground into which domestic waste was tipped once a week. Bill and Annie rummaged through the recent arrivals looking for old tins and any scraps of food they could find. What an utterly miserable existence they must have had. How could we have been so mean as to laugh and jeer at them as they passed through the centre of the village?

The Scandal Beck, a tributary of the River Eden which flows through the middle of Soulby, is enveloped on either side by about 2 acres of village green. This made for a wonderful playground. Football was played on most days. Our coats or jumpers were laid on the grass to act as goal mouths. Frank Walton, our landlord, had his joinery workshop on one side of the green. The resinous smell of newly sawn timber wafted over the pitch. The ball occasionally smashed the glass in his workshop window and this didn't go down at all well with old Frank. If he was in his workshop, he would amble out of the door and demand the ball from us before the first kick. 'Bring the ball, bring the ball,' he would call out in his slow, drawling monotone voice.

In his spare time, Frank was a Methodist lay preacher. He was such an important person in the village and held in such high respect by all the adults that we always obeyed his demands.

The same respect wasn't shown to Stan Pratt. Stan and Nellie Pratt lived in a cottage next to Frank's workshop. Stan worked for the council on the roads. He and Freddie Jackson from Crosby Garrett were employed as lengthmen, a term used for workers who were responsible for certain sections of road where they lived. Often they worked together and used the same workmen's hut situated near the bridge over the Scandal Beck. The hut had a solid fuel fire around which Stan and Freddie would spend many an hour keeping warm and drinking tea. One of the pranks which gave us boys the most fun was to smoke Stan and Freddie out of their hut. This we did by putting grass sods over the top of the chimney. By the time our cunning plan had caused them to choke and rush to the door for air, we were well hidden, but able to watch with great merriment.

One day, a group of us were playing down by the river when Stan happened to walk past. Jimmy Moffatt, who was about five years older than me, ran up to Stan, snatched his cap off his head and threw it in the river. Stan went ballistic and dived towards young Moffatt. Flying horizontally through the air a mere 2 feet from the ground, he grabbed the boy's ankles, sending him crashing to the ground. He ended up half in the water and half on dry land. Shaking with rage, Stan yanked Jimmy upright before kicking him up the backside whilst shouting at him in Westmorland dialect, 'Git cu back I heven't finished wi the yit' (which loosely meant *Go away, no, I have changed my mind. Come back, because I haven't finished with you yet*). Jimmy was terrified and fled the scene with great haste. Of course, he didn't dare tell his parents about this experience, for in those days they would have given him a good hiding for being cheeky and disrespectful to an adult.

The Bennett family consisted of Martha; her husband, Willie; their three children and their grandma, Mrs Slinger. They were regular victims of us village pranksters. The favourite trick we played on them was to tie a long piece of thread to their door knocker at dusk. Holding on to the other end of the thread, we hid behind the stone wall which surrounded their front garden. A few tugs of the thread and the Bennetts would get a knock on the front door. When they answered the door to non-existent visitors, we couldn't always control our giggles. It was a harmless enough jape but one which never failed to amuse us.

Chores, some more pleasant than others, were part of our childhood. Picking rose hips was a tedious chore. The thorns tore your hands and any bare flesh they grabbed. The wild rose bushes weren't always easy to reach. Branches often had to be pulled down with a stick. The trick was to hold the stick with one hand and pick the hips with the other. Branches would often spring back. The stick would fly into the air, the picker left bloodied and hipless. It seemed to take forever to pick a pound of rose hips. For every pound, we got 4d (4 old pence).

Once a week during the picking season, we took our haul to my Auntie Vara and Uncle Joe's. They ran the village post office. Auntie Vara took in sewing and Uncle Joe worked at Kirkby Stephen auction mart. To further supplement their income, they were the village gathering point for rose hips. Hips were weighed, the pickers then paid and the hips put into long, narrow hessian sacks. A Newcastle firm called Scott and Nephew did a weekly collection. They turned the hips into vitamin C-rich rose-hip syrup. Children were dosed up with this rather sickly, thick elixir on a regular basis in order to keep colds and scurvy at bay.

Gathering wild mushrooms was an altogether more pleasant and lucrative task. It was, however, very unpredictable. How many grew in the fields varied greatly from year to year. Fields in which horses had grazed were the best. Plenty of horse manure led to lots of mushrooms. What I didn't know then was that the number of mushrooms is also very dependent on weather conditions in late summer/autumn. Warmth, moisture in the soil and humidity make for happy spores and plentiful mushies.

We got to the fields armed with cardboard boxes in early morning. Rather like football supporters striding out to the match with heads held high and bright, smiling faces, we always expected to be onto a winner and go home with overflowing baskets. If there weren't many, we, like the footy fans, would trudge back home with our miserable faces almost on the ground.

A few mushrooms were eaten at home. Mam used to poach them in a little milk. She was always keen to give us healthy food. Tasty fry-ups were a rarity at Lilac Cottage.

The bulk of the harvest was taken to Kirkby Stephen. Busloads of Geordies used Kirkby as a stop-off point between Newcastle and the seaside resorts of Morecambe and Blackpool. The era of cheap foreign holidays hadn't arrived. Nowadays, Tenerife and Benidorm would most likely be their destinations of choice.

Fortunately, they couldn't get enough of our tasty mushrooms. They paid handsomely too, around 2 shillings and sixpence a boxful as I remember.

***

What we bought, how we bought it and where we bought it in the 1950s bears very little resemblance to today's shopping experiences.

During my early years growing up in Soulby, there was a village shop, which went under the rather grand title of Soulby County Stores. Mr and Mrs Gardener were the shopkeepers. Nat was highly regarded for his photography skills. I still have two of the photographs he took of me.

They are a reminder of my curly locks. I looked so angelic, sat on a tree stump in one, and on an upturned tin bucket with a cushion under my bum in the other. My parents and grandparents regularly purchased a range of items at the shop, but not the bulk of the food items.

The monthly shop for groceries was obtained from Hastwells of Kirkby Stephen. On the last Monday of the month, Dick Birtles of Hastwells would visit to take the monthly order. He would sit down at the living room table armed with a notepad and pencil. After being given a cup of tea (always Typhoo), he would begin with general pleasantries and ask about the health and welfare of all the family members. Then it was down to business, which involved Dick jogging the customers' memories by running through a list of all the items Mother or Grandmother regularly bought.

'How are you for tea, Mrs Haigh?' or Mrs Longstaff in my grandmother's case.

'Better have four quarter pound packets of Typhoo, please, Dick,' was the usual reply.

Tea bags hadn't been invented back then.

'Do you need any Rich Tea biscuits? How much flour would you like this month?' was the general pattern of this order-taking.

I guess you could compare this with today's online shopping, but sadly the internet equivalent lacks the personal touch. Dick Birtles' visit was a social event which was marked on the calendar. Two days after the regular ordering ritual, Hastwells' lorry would deliver the groceries. Everything was neatly packed in brown paper bags with handwritten labels and these were transported in cardboard boxes. Yes, plastic bags hadn't been invented; excessive wrapping with sell-by and use-by dates didn't exist, so there was no problem regarding environmental pollution.

The butcher's van visited the village every Friday, driven by my Uncle James, the proprietor. The business, which was started by my grandfather, John (Jack) Longstaff, hence the name J. Longstaff and Son – High-Class Family Butcher.

Uncle James was accompanied by Ernie Warwick, his long-time faithful right-hand man. In warm weather, the back door of the van was left open as it moved slowly and steadily through the village. Presumably to prevent the meat getting too hot, as there was no refrigerated transport in the 1950s. Ernie sat in the back with his legs dangling out. Both vehicle and occupants went at a much slower pace of life back then, so there was no risk of Warwick or the meat getting thrown about. When they served each customer, Uncle James took the order and Ernie cut the meat, weighed it and wrapped it in paper. Uncle James took the money. The range of meats sold was like the range of groceries, very limited compared with today's vast offerings. There would be joints for Sunday roasts, including mutton, which I found to be of very rank flavour; Cumberland sausages; bacon and potted meat, a concoction of fatty oddments cooked up in a big electric boiler. Potted meat was disgusting. It had small bits of bone in it which felt like grit held together in a greasy, wobbly mass. Cheap meat, but to my tastebuds it was unfit to eat. My brother, who took over the business from Uncle James, was still making potted meat until 2008. The current proprietor may still make and sell it. I haven't the slightest desire to find out.

Ice cream is the one taste I would love to travel back in time for. Beleza really was Italian. He made the most delicious ice cream I have ever tasted. The mere thought of it after sixty plus years is enough to instigate the most extreme cravings. How did we get Italian ice cream in Soulby? For a start, it's a wonder they allowed a foreigner into the village. How it began I don't know, but once his ice cream had been tasted, he was probably made a freeman of Soulby.

Beleza, who hailed from Darlington, would in his Noddy-style ice cream van visit Soulby and neighbouring villages once a week. Down the hill, playing a rapid, jerky, repetitive tune (not an Italian classic), Beleza's van would arrive at 4.30 pm. We were beside ourselves with anticipation. Jerking about as children do and getting under the feet of adults was part of the build-up to our cones, or wafers if we had enough pocket money.

At the first sight and sound of the van, we would excitedly shout in our high-pitched infants' voices, 'Beleza's here, Beleza's here,' and run to where the van always stopped near the bridge. Jostling for position at the front of the queue and holding our money in sticky little hands, we gabbled out our requests. No matter how hyped up we were, we never forgot to say please and thank you.

***

What seemed like weeks of preparation went into the construction of the village bonfire. All the boys of Soulby would collect any piece of timber available in this mammoth task, with the sole aim of making the bonfire the biggest yet.

Bit by bit, a massive, or so it seemed to us, cone-shaped stack would rise up from the earth on the village green, a few feet away from the River Scandal. For many years, I wondered how this small beck got such a notorious name. I was quite disappointed when I found out that the truth had nothing to do with foul deeds, crimes or adultery committed by any notable parishioners. Apparently, in this case, the name "Scandal" is derived from two Old Norse words meaning "short valley".

Each year, the bonfire was shrouded in the same controversy, instigated by nearby residents who worried over wayward sparks setting light to their property. Understandably, the villager who protested most loudly was Tom Brass, whose farm was only about 50 yards away. A strong wind could quite easily have fanned the flames towards his hay barn. However, had the worst happened, I'm quite sure Tom could have dealt with it all by himself without the aid of the fire brigade. Tom, you see, was something of a champion when it came to spitting. I can still see this enormous figure, over 6 feet tall with very broad shoulders, sitting in one corner of his farmhouse living room and delivering with awesome power and accuracy mouthfuls of spit onto the coal fire. This disgusting habit was part of Tom's pipe-smoking technique and was in those days considered to be quite normal. A barn fire, oh yes, I'm sure Tom would have had it sizzling to submission in no time. Anyway, despite his annual protestations, Soulby's bonfire always went ahead.

For a few days before Bonfire Night we took a Guy Fawkes around the village. It was made from old clothes and straw with a hollowed-out turnip (swede actually) for a head. A candle in the head illuminated it very effectively. The Guy was sat in a four-wheeled bogey made from an old pram or some similar discarded mode of transport. Every house was visited whether we were welcome or not. The younger children, including myself, stayed some distance away from the front doors of people who we knew did not like us, like Ned Cowperthwaite. Ned was a fearsome-looking old man with bloodshot eyes who always snarled at children. We were petrified of him, but that didn't stop us teasing and tormenting him from a safe distance. Knocking on doors and asking for money (a penny for the guy?) was left to the big boys like my brother, John, and his friends Jimmy Moffat, Tom Moffat, Harold Birkbeck and Geoffrey Bainbridge. In order to justify this begging and prise money out of the locals, we always sang this little ditty –

"A rope – a rope to hang the Pope,
A penorth of cheese to choke him
A bottle of beer to wash it down
And Soulby Pump to soak him."

The money collected from this entertainment extravaganza was used to buy a few fireworks. Pretty mild stuff compared to today's pyrotechnics. Still, it amused us and was almost always harmless fun. I guess the few older people we frightened with bangers would disagree.

As for fireworks, we kept them at home in the sideboard. What would the health and safety nerds think about that now? By the time Bonfire Night arrived, there can't have been much gunpowder left in them. Almost every day they would be taken out of the sideboard, placed on the living room floor and counted with much admiration and expectancy.

When the great night finally arrived, we wore warm waterproof clothing. It seemed to bucket it down almost every year. On the village green, there were always heated technical discussions on how best to light the Great Fire of Soulby. As far as I can remember, some old diesel from one of the farms was thrown on and then lit with a long taper.

Then the fun really began. Rockets were lit, many failing to get more than a few feet off the ground, Catherine Wheels refused to spin, but the Mount Vesuvius and Golden Showers always lived up to expectations.

As the flames died down, potatoes were placed in the hot embers. We couldn't wait for them to cook through properly so they were always black on the outside and rock hard inside, but bravely we told each other how delicious they were.

After all the weeks of excited build-up, Bonfire Night was over for another year. It only lasted about one and a half hours. Still, for a good few days we could see the smouldering ash and scorched grass, and these images gave us something to cling to as we looked forward to next year's celebrations. I don't suppose Guy Fawkes had any idea his crime would have created so much pleasure throughout the land, and would have had such a lasting impact on the 200 or so residents of this small Westmorland village.

***

"The Band of Hope" may sound like the name of a late '50s or early '60s pop group, but actually it was the collective name for an organisation of anti-alcohol zealots. Now known simply as "Hope", readers can find out more about its history and aims at Hopeuk.org. Sparsely populated Westmorland seemed to have a preponderance of teetotal self-righteous fanatics in my early years.

Soulby's Methodist Chapel was the regular meeting place for these God-fearing tub-thumpers, who tried to put the fear of the Almighty into old and young alike by denouncing the evils of drink. Alcohol had no place in our house. "When drink's in, wit's out", was one of my mother's frequently quoted mantras.

Leslie Harris, a Methodist lay preacher and joiner from the nearby village of Winton, was the chief purveyor of the perils to be encountered by anyone who so much as smelt any alcoholic liquid. Sharply dressed in a buff tweed suit and highly polished brogues, Mr Harris was like an early version of the American evangelist Billy Graham and amassed a large fan club of dedicated followers in the upper Eden Valley. The older generation of church-

or chapel-going villagers had a very simplistic view of good and bad or right and wrong. Anyone who imbibed was condemned as an alcoholic. They were considered shameful and worthless individuals who were on a fast track to the abyss, where they would end up penniless and destitute.

Leslie's persuasive tongue and handwritten signs, with such simple fundamental messages as *Drinking alcohol is a SIN*, interspersed his sermons to such a terrifying extent that it was no wonder the village public house was closed in Soulby. Mr Harris was a marvellous performer with a large following. It was a good job he worked for good and not evil, because some villagers were very gullible and anxious for a hero to worship.

As children, we liked the Band of Hope, not because of its crusade against the dreaded drink, but due to the fact that each year in May/June, it organised a carnival called the *Demonstration*. There were precious few social events to look forward to, and this was by far the biggest and best. This jamboree took place in the market town of Kirkby Stephen one year and in Appleby, the county town of Westmorland, the next year, always on a Saturday. Each village in Westmorland assembled at the railway station at 10.30 am under its own banner. These were massive colourful placards resembling those used by the miners' unions. At the head of the parade was the local silver band playing with pomp and ceremony as it led the procession to the playing field at the other side of town.

Once on the playing field, the separate village groups would take up their allotted space of grass. Trestle tables were erected and laid with sandwiches, cakes, soft drinks and tea or coffee (for the adults). Jelly and trifle would follow later in the afternoon.

The major attraction of the day was the funfair. This created much excitement amongst the children. There was no holding us back. Chattering incoherently, we would race off to the roundabouts.

Waltzers and dodgem cars were too big and scary for the small boys and girls, the joys of which were only to be enjoyed by the big children. Screeches of delight could be heard above the distorted sound of the pop tunes of the day. Elvis Presley, Buddy Holly and Cliff Richard blasting out from the loudspeakers – the atmosphere created was truly memorable. It is so easy to recreate in the mind the sounds and sights of those special bygone times. Coconut shies, dart stalls, pellet guns and magnetic fishing rods, where goldfish and cuddly toys could be won, all added up to this grand day out.

Later in the day, it was time for sports events. Inter-village football, the sack race, the egg and spoon and three-legged races were part of the healthy physical activities, good for mind and soul. On one occasion, the sack race ended in hilarious failure. A manically yapping Jack Russell Terrier ran across the track and sank its teeth into the sack of the race leader. With exceptional strength, it pulled the young boy inside the sack over. He looked petrified. All the other competitors broke into hysterical laughter. The race had to be run again, but nobody cared about the result. Patch the dog was the outright winner that year.

By about 5.30 pm, happy but exhausted, it was time to pack up and go home. *Demonstration Day* was over for another year. Well, not really. For the older children (late teens) and adults, it had only just begun.

Teenagers were allowed to stay up much later. My first time as a teenager was a shocking eye-opener. It was then that I saw for myself what really went on as the sun went down on *Demonstration Day*. Looking back, I think it was the first time I had seen adults staggering about and slurring their words. What a shock to discover that knowingly or not, the Band of Hope's big event had been taken over by adults who had frequented the public houses. I even witnessed a drunken fight between two older boys, probably over a girl.

The words of Leslie Harris came rushing back into my brain. He was right all along; drink really was a demon. Then I thought, *But surely the organisers must know what happens late in the day and every year.* Oh yes, they knew all right, but the drunks spent loads of money, which helped the coffers of the Band of Hope. Talk about double standards. Still, Leslie Harris was probably sitting at home drinking a double Scotch (I have no evidence of this whatsoever; that's just my mischievous imagination) in celebration of another successful *Demonstration Day*.

Four

Leather Balls and Rattles

Named after the hamlet of Waitby, the "Waitby Cup" was a knockout football competition played every spring by villages in the Upper Eden Valley district of Westmorland.

Every village played on the flattest field available. This depended on the permission of the farmer who owned the land. The quality of the playing surface left much to be desired. When, as was often the case, there was a good covering of cow pats, this favoured the defenders. If sliding tackles were timed to perfection, the shit-covered ground offered less resistance. As the opposing forward fell to the ground, he would get splattered all over with the sloshy, smelly brown stuff. Farmers' sons and farmworkers filled most positions in every team, so the muck bothered them not a jot.

Soulby's pitch was fairly good, but none of them bore the slightest comparison to the professionally manicured, weed-free hallowed turf of Wembley or any professional pitch at even the lowest level.

When it wasn't being played on, our village pitch was a cow pasture. The grass contained vigorous forage species, like ryegrass. Growing in amongst the grasses would be buttercups and often a few nettles and thistles. The grass wasn't cut before matches. The farmer got his priorities right. His field was a source of good-quality food for his cattle. It was through his generosity that there was any type of field for the team. Our village was lucky to have a reasonably level pitch. Even so, grass length varied throughout the pitch, and the cattle hoofprints meant the ball would bounce off the uneven surface in a very unpredictable manner.

This was grassroots football in its heyday in the 1950s. The Waitby Cup is still going, but in a much-diminished format. Matches were played mid-week during April and May. Day length had to allow the games, which kicked off at 7.30 pm, to be completed before it became too dark. There were no changing rooms. A barn or byre sufficed. Half-time refreshments were brought to the side of the pitch. Half an orange was each player's ration.

Players wore heavy leather boots which came halfway up their ankles. Studs were nailed onto the bottom of the boots to help grip on the grassy surface. Shin pads made from corrugated cardboard were stuffed down the stockings. This was a cheap means of avoiding a broken leg. Waitby Cup footballers took no prisoners.

Footballs consisted of a rubber bladder encased in a heavy leather cover. After the bladder was inflated, the leather outer was laced up. Evidence now points to brain damage and dementia amongst some former professional players caused by heading these heavy early balls. When wet, the ball, like the boots, became much, much weightier. Playing ninety minutes on a rough pitch with those heavy balls and boots must have been totally exhausting for even the fittest Waitby Cup footballer. The relief felt at the end of each game by friends and relatives was palpable.

***

With receding hair, of medium build and a scant 5ft 7ins tall, Dad was a very talented footballer. He was an inside forward, whose vision and skilful caressing of the ball could unlock the most uncompromising defence. He was by all accounts the star player in Soulby's team. It was said that if he had been spotted by a talent scout and been given the opportunity, he could have played for a professional club. Using today's over-hyped football language, he would most likely have become a legend. Sadly, the scouting tentacles of Manchester or even Carlisle United didn't extend as far as this remote farming area.

The Cup Final was held at Hills Bottom on the banks of the River Eden in Kirkby Stephen. This would have been the best playing surface for miles around. Even so, the old black and white photographs show the teams posing amongst attractive wild flowers. So far as the monocultural world of sports turf is concerned, such flora

Waitby Cup 1938
Furniss Haigh seciond from the left in front row

is not to be tolerated. The kit worn consisted of thick, black knee-length shorts and shirts with a black and beige squared pattern.

I have two photographs of my dad taken when Soulby won the cup. One has 1938 in white letters painted on the ball. It was nine years before I was born; Dad was thirty-two; my sister, Joyce, who was ten years older than me, was a baby. My Uncle James, the team captain, proudly holds the cup with my dad next to him. The other photo doesn't have a date, but it must have been about two years previous, because one of the team was James Henderson, a relative on my grandmother's side. He was killed in the Second World War. I think the competition was suspended during the war (1939-1945). The final piece of evidence of my dad's playing career that I possess is a winner's medal from 1951 when he was forty-five years old. Furniss Haigh had a long and distinguished career. He never lost his love of the game and was a lifelong supporter of Leeds United, his home team.

***

My brother was, like his father, a star of Soulby's Waitby Cup teams. During his twenty-year playing career, he amassed five winners' cups as well as three runner-up medals.

Though I never saw my father play, I did see my brother terrorising his opponents on numerous occasions. It was said that John didn't have Dad's silky skills. He was a more direct player who loved to score. When he galloped down the wing, many a fullback was left floundering in his wake. Many goals came from his right boot, with which he struck the ball with venom and lethal accuracy. "Stop Haighy and we have a chance of beating Soulby," seemed to be the mantra of the opposition.

The professional game is now far removed from the era of my childhood. Pitch management has evolved with research into the most suitable hard-wearing grass species which ensures a smooth dense sward. Turf nutrition, pest and disease control and expensive sophisticated machinery make grounds maintenance a precise science. Advanced drainage systems and underground heating means ideal playing surfaces all the year round. Footballs are lighter, available in any colour and made from polyurethane. In comparison to the old boots, the modern ones are akin to slippers.

Supporters pay extortionate prices to watch their over-paid and over-hyped heroes. I wonder, do they get the same level of excitement that we got watching our village teams going for glory? No, they most certainly do not. Village rivalry was intense but good-natured. There was no bad language or fighting between opposing supporters. Crowds were large and very animated. Most of the village was standing near the touchline. Rattles whirred and every pass and shot was either cheered or booed. We all looked forward with joyful anticipation to the thrill of seeing our team holding aloft the Waitby Cup.

***

In 1963, when I was sixteen, John and I went to our first professional football match. His dark blue second-hand Triumph Herald with the number plate DOS 88 coughed and spluttered its way to Carlisle United's Brunton Park. It was a lovely, warm spring evening, and Carlisle had to win to get promotion to the 2nd division. This they did in spectacular fashion, beating Mansfield by 5 goals to 1. We were snared.

The old ground was packed out. I had never seen so many people in one place. We stood in an old wooden stand called the "scratching shed". The setting sun flickered across the lush turf and picked out the thousands of beaming, excited and expectant faces in the crowd. It was such an intoxicating event. The crowd clapped and cheered every Carlisle pass, shot and save. I can still recite the name of every player in that team. It was the last match of the season. We wished there wasn't to be a summer break.

Over the next four years, we went to almost every home game. Mam didn't approve and couldn't stop telling us that we should be doing something useful with our spare time rather than watching silly football. There wasn't time in her virtuous life for leisure and pleasure.

Once, we went on a coach to see Carlisle take on the mighty Newcastle United in the FA Cup at St James' Park. The crowd numbered 56,000. This was around 40,000 more than I had ever seen at Carlisle. As the ground filled up and expectation grew, the crowd swayed back and forth. The blue scarves of Carlisle outnumbered four to one by the black and white of Newcastle. The rapid whirring of rattles being swung above so many heads built up to a crescendo as kick-off approached. One of our group, Maurice, was wearing a dark blue duffle coat. When another fan brushed past him, a toggle from Maurice's coat got entangled with a button from the other man's coat. Maurice was dragged down the terraces for some distance before both men stopped and were able to free themselves. Maurice scrambled his way back up the steps to rejoin us. His face had a sickly pallor as a result of this terrifying ordeal. This freak occurrence could have ended in serious injury for either or both supporters.

Once the game got underway, all eyes were on Newcastle's tall, ginger-haired, Welsh international centre-forward called Wynn Davies. Newcastle fans sang their own version of Manfred Mann's *Mighty Quinn* with *Wynn* instead of *Quinn*. They expected him to score a hatful against lowly Carlisle. Against all odds, the unthinkable happened when after ten minutes, the smallest player on the pitch, Carlisle's Tommy Murray at 5ft 4in, scored with a header. It was the only goal of the game. In celebration of this famous victory, copious amounts of beer were consumed on the bus back home. I only had one bottle and managed on that occasion not to incur my mam's wrath for imbibing the demon drink.

We enjoyed many exciting games at Brunton Park as well as a fair smattering of tedious encounters. Most of the latter occurred towards the end of every season against opposition who, like Carlisle, were sitting in mid-table mediocrity. In the words of Frank, a fellow regular supporter, 'We would have been better off at home with toothache.'

Five

Five Rollercoaster Years End on a High

Never before had I experienced the bliss of being able to lie at full stretch in a white bath with both cold and hot water on tap. The embarrassing Friday night ritual of squeezing into the tin bath in front of the fire was consigned to the Haigh family's history book.

It was late 1959, and I was eleven years old when we moved into Inglenook. My Grandma Ada, Alice Longstaff, died, aged seventy-eight on the 4th of March that year. Her house was my mother's inheritance. With one short move across the village, we became a property-owning family. Our new house had a living room, a sitting room, kitchen, pantry, three bedrooms and of course the bathroom. Had we owned a car, it would have been like trading in a Reliant Robin for a Jaguar.

Mam had longed for this day for a very long time. She acutely felt the stigma of not owning her own home. Most residents of Soulby were owner-occupiers. No longer were we at the mercy of Frank Walton the Methodist businessman, who collected the rent but seemed oblivious to the need to carry out even the most basic property maintenance. The only time he set foot in Lilac Cottage was to sweep the chimney – a job for which he got additional pay.

The new bathroom at Inglenook had been built by Willie Fairer, a builder from Warcop. With my tiny wooden wheelbarrow getting under his feet, I must have been a real nuisance. Thoughts of old Frank never disappeared, because Grandma had then paid Frank the joiner to make an airing cupboard. Every time you switched the immersion heater on or off, Frank's all-too-rustic carpentry skills could be seen in stark relief. His level of skill was far better suited to making five bar farm gates held together with 6-inch nails. Still, I have nothing to boast about, having never created anything from timber which could even remotely be classed as elegant.

The year we moved house was the year I started secondary school. Kitted out in my maroon blazer and grey flannels, I got on the school bus for the first time. It was the start of the autumn term. I had to travel two miles to Kirkby Stephen Grammar School.

As I entered the main building, I felt totally overawed. After Soulby School, the place seemed massive. Every subject had its own classroom. There was a gymnasium (a building which I hated in my first two years), an assembly hall and a dining room. Finding my way around, meeting all the new teachers and being given a timetable to follow was all too much to absorb. For the first week I wandered around in a state of complete bewilderment. I felt as if I was dropping into a sinkhole with no one I knew to pull me to safety.

Due to my lack of academic achievement, I was placed in the class below the clever pupils. Once I got the hang of the Big School, I felt under no pressure and enjoyed my first year. The one exception being Gymnastics, which was taught by a bullying Scotsman called Mr Tate. He yelled out instructions like a sergeant major and seemed to take a sadistic pleasure if you couldn't climb the ropes or jump over the wooden horse. He was in his element as he caused great embarrassment when teaching the boys and girls to dance together. In all other subjects, I was highly commended for my hard work. To my surprise and my parents' delight, I was promoted into the top division for the start of the second year.

There was, in my view, one major drawback resulting from my elevation. This was the change in some of the subjects. In the first year, I took Rural Studies. Taught by a genial, country-loving teacher called Teddy Relph (an expert in Westmorland dialect), the hands-on care of animals and plants was the crux of this subject. I loved it. I could see the point of it. We were allowed to feel, touch and nurture living things. I also enjoyed Pottery, although I never really mastered the art of pot throwing. Rural Studies and Pottery were not taught in the top stream. They were subjects for the thick pupils.

My first two terms in the top stream were on the whole successful. However, by the end of the summer term, my enthusiasm and effort began to wane. Latin stands out as a classic example of this demise. I had been in the top six in a class of about thirty until I was persuaded to help another pupil (Peter Myers) with his homework. When we handed it in, it was identical. Mr Fryer, our Latin teacher, was a big, hefty hulk (fat in other words) from St Helens with slicked-back Brylcreemed hair. Not the kind of man to annoy.

Sitting behind his desk with our exercise books in front of him, he bawled out, 'I smell a rat. Haigh and Myers, come to the front. Bring my slipper, Haigh.'

He didn't actually lather us, he didn't need to. The threat of doing so was enough. Although my Latin doesn't reach the same standard as it did in the early months, it has always stood me in good stead when learning botanical plant names and what they mean.

During the rest of my time at grammar school, my scholastic endeavours were noted more for my resounding failures than for the few minor successes. Doing homework was met with stubborn resistance. Mam would insist on me spending so many hours in my bedroom doing my homework. Most of that time I did very little work and just sat there bored rigid, staring into space.

The biggest disappointment for her must have been my Music mock O-level result. I amassed the grand total of 1% – a record which probably stands to this day. Physics, I didn't try to understand. Chemistry, with all those glass bottles full of spluttering, bubbling acids, scared me witless.

History and Geography were all right, but weren't taught in a very engaging way. Maths I genuinely found difficult to fathom. English Language was one of my few successes, because I found it easy and could see how useful it was.

Sport became more enjoyable once the dreaded Mr Tate left. His replacement, whose name I can't recall, gave me the nickname of Whisky. It was amazing what being recognised did for my self-esteem. I was selected for the college soccer team and the rugby team. My rugby position was hooker and my job was to get the ball with my feet when it was thrown into the scrum. What success I had was down to fear. I reasoned that if I got in the first kick (not on the ball, but on the opposition hooker), he would often back out of the challenge. It was a case of kick first or be kicked.

The Rugby League-loving Mr Fryer took us on a couple of day trips to see professional rugby matches. On one occasion, we went to Whitehaven to see the home side play Fryer's beloved St Helens. St Helens had a resounding victory and Teacher was overjoyed. On the other occasion, we went in a minibus to Millom to play in some inter-school tournament. The date was the 22nd of November 1963. On the minibus radio, the programme was interrupted by a sombre message that President John F Kennedy had been shot and killed. It is the only thing I remember from that trip.

I left school on Wednesday, 25th March 1964. My mock O-level results were so poor that it was suggested I needn't bother staying to take the actual exams. This advice became more forcibly delivered when a careers adviser asked me what I wanted to do upon leaving school. 'Be a gardener,' I said, without hesitation.

'Oh, well, you may as well leave now and get a job, as you don't need any qualifications to be a farmer,' was the ignorant retort. I didn't question this remark. What would have been the point of querying someone's advice who didn't know the difference between agriculture and horticulture? However, leaving school without any qualifications was largely down to my laziness. This was a situation I began to rectify three years later. It wasn't a question of being a late developer, more a case of realising that needs must.

***

Soon after we moved to Inglenook, a change in Dad's working pattern meant he lived at home seven nights a week. Although still employed by the railway, he no longer had to travel to Ribblehead Viaduct. His work became much nearer to home and within daily travelling distance.

He bought a BSA Bantam 125cc motorcycle. This small, low-powered bike was a two-stroke, which meant it ran off a mixture of petrol and oil. After putting the ingredients in the tank, he would shake the machine from side to side. This caused the fuel to swirl around and mix thoroughly. Then it was time to kick-start the engine. Two or three partial depressions of the starting lever with his right foot and a murmuring, mechanical sound would be heard. Dad followed his first tentative kicks with a more vigorous total depression. Often, this was followed by a grumbling tut. It usually took a few kicks and many of Dad's tuts before the little bike limped into life with a quiet brum, brum, brum when he opened the throttle.

Clad in an army coat, my dad straddled the machine. The wearing of crash helmets was not a legal requirement. Dad wore a tight-fitting flat cap when riding his motorbike. In order to prevent a gust of wind blowing his cap off, he rode with his head facing downwards. This meant his field of vision was very limited. Amazingly, despite this dangerous practice, he never had an accident. A clicking sound signalled the clutch being pulled in followed by a clank as he pressed the gear lever down into first with his right foot. With the clutch released, off he went – put, put, put.

He must have been delighted to have the luxury of home comforts every night. I really got to know my father for the first time. When previously I had only seen him at weekends, it always seemed a bit like meeting a stranger on Friday nights. We became much more relaxed together.

Working on the railways had its share of dangers. My dad was first on the scene after a fellow worker had been struck by a passing train in Blea Moor Tunnel. This man was killed instantly. Mam told us about this accident, but my dad was so affected by this tragedy that he couldn't bring himself to even mention it. We knew it was best not to ask him about it.

After his move to a small gang close to home, we felt there was less risk of accidents. Then on a summer's day in 1961, disaster struck. Dad was working at Appleby Station.

Not on the railway line, but in the station yard. All those years spent in a cage at the side of Ribblehead Viaduct and he came to no harm. Then, in one reckless moment when (under the instructions of the foreman) the gang were carrying out an unapproved risky manoeuvre which involved hitching a trailer to a lorry, Dad was run over by the lorry. It crushed his pelvis and did severe damage to his bladder.

I was hit by the news when I came home from school. Looking ashen, with tears in her eyes, my mam's trembling voice said, 'Your dad's had an accident and is in Cumberland Infirmary. It's very serious, so bad he may not survive. He's had an operation, but it's too early to say if it's been successful. You and John are going to have to be very brave.' Mam made regular phone calls to the infirmary that night from the kiosk in the centre of the village. However, this tragedy hastened the arrival of our own telephone.

Next day, the hospital said he had pulled through the operation but that we should go to see him, because it was still touch and go. John drove us there in his not-so-reliable Triumph Herald, but we made it for afternoon visiting hours. It was daily 80-mile round trips to Carlisle for the next couple of weeks. Dad had a sturdy constitution and a very strong heart. He made an excellent recovery and was sent home in the third week.

However, his bladder had been very severely damaged and so he soon had to return to hospital for another operation to improve the flow from his bladder. After the first operation, we thought this was to be a minor routine event. It didn't turn out quite so straightforward, because this time around, Dad got a clot of blood on his lung. Again, he skirted with death. Regular journeys were made to hospital.

This time, John couldn't drive. John was a teddy boy. He had the clothes, drainpipe trousers and winkle pickers, and was often involved in the obligatory fights. One night, he broke the leader finger in his right hand which made driving impossible. Jossie Sowerby, a very kind neighbour of advancing years, kindly offered to do the driving. Jossie's old bloodshot eyes were not the most efficient at judging distance and focussing on detail. In other words, he was too blind to drive safely. How we got there and back on several occasions without an accident was more than lucky. But we did, and in a few more weeks Dad was back home. He was fifty-three and never worked again.

He made regular visits to hospital as an outpatient for many years to come. On most occasions, this meant a long, tiring round trip to Newcastle, where the facilities and staff were better able to deal with his bladder problems than was the case at Carlisle. It was a painful procedure which obviously took its toll, but Dad never moaned.

What upset him most of all was his inability to work. He felt useless, I guess largely because he couldn't provide for his family. The railway company did eventually pay compensation, which gave us financial security. This didn't relieve the frustration he felt being trapped at home every day. John took him for trips in his car and after I passed my test I did the same in my mini-van. His favourite places were in the Yorkshire Dales. That, for him, was going back home. It was working on the railway which brought him from Pateley Bridge to Kirkby Stephen where he met my mam, who was born and brought up just outside Soulby. The railway was responsible for two life-changing events in my dad's life.

***

Although I had always felt a real closeness to the soil and loved, and still do love, getting my hands dirty, I, like most boys, dabbled with the idea of being a train driver, or a builder. At one period, the idea of being a journalist had a strong appeal. Moving to Inglenook put all such notions out of my head. We had a proper garden at Inglenook. From that day forward, I knew I was going to be a gardener. I faced no family opposition to this ambition. I guess it was thought I would soon get over this latest fad.

John was keen to follow in the Longstaff family tradition with his love of farming and the butchery trade. Dad said very little. Unless he got angry, that was the way he was. Mam's not-too-subtle way of trying to knock my horticultural enthusiasm was to say, 'Mr Meads thinks you would make a very good vicar. That would make me very proud of you.' But I was not to be pushed off the garden path. Where and how to begin turning the garden of Inglenook into a botanical wonderland was my all-consuming vision.

The narrow space between the front of the house and the road was the obvious place to start. Youthful enthusiasm pushed any thought of the possibility of failure clean out of my mind. Grandma's much-cherished old herbaceous plants were decrepit and there was no room for them. Without sentiment, I threw them out. My replacements – hybrid tea and floribunda roses – were at the top of the plant charts in the late '50s and '60s. I needed to know what to do with the soil and how to grow roses.

For answers to these and many other gardening questions, I consulted the guru. I got a copy of *Mr Middleton's Garden Book*. He was the Monty Don of his day – a keen amateur who became the first BBC television and radio gardener. I absorbed all the information and then thought I knew everything. Well-rotted farmyard manure was dug into the ground several weeks before planting. Fertiliser was added at planting, and Mr Middleton's little drawings on the method of planting were consulted. I received a pair of secateurs and a small sprayer as presents. To grow the perfect blemish-free roses you had to apply chemicals at regular intervals. This was the era when anything which moved in the garden was considered a pest. The vast array of pesticides and fungicides were an essential part of the armoury serious gardeners used to defeat the enemy.

When it came to selecting which roses to grow, I sent off for a catalogue from the top rose breeder. Sam McGredy was the fourth generation of rose growers from Portadown in Northern Ireland. I hovered behind the letterbox every morning for what seemed days, waiting for the postman to deliver my catalogue. When he did, I thought all my birthdays had arrived at once. The catalogue was jam-packed with glossy photos and hints on getting the best from McGredy's roses. There was only room for ten or so bush roses and two ramblers over the front door. How could I possibly choose the best varieties?

My first choice was "Peace", so named in 1945 as the Second World War came to an end. It is still regarded by many as the finest hybrid tea rose ever raised. For the ramblers, I chose "American Pillar". Other varieties picked included "Wendy Cussons" and "Iceberg". I paid meticulous attention to detail when it came to caring for my roses. From the first year after planting until I left home nine years later, the rose garden received much acclaim.

However, a much less flamboyant plant set my gardening genes on fire. It was none other than the humble cabbage. I sowed a packet, yes! – a whole packet of cabbage seeds. Hundreds appeared, and this wonder of nature had me spellbound. I still experience the same magical thrill when seeds germinate and cuttings root.

'What will you do with all those little plants?' asked my mam.

'Sell them!' I said, without any idea as to how, where and who would buy them. More in hope than expectation, I put a marketing card in the sitting room window. *Cabbage plants for sale, 2 shillings and sixpence per score* was the no-frills sales ploy I employed. To everyone's surprise in the family, including mine, I sold out of plants within a week. *Well, that's it*, I thought, *this gardening game is definitely for me. If I can grow plants so easily and sell them, that's brilliant.* So many people think that raising and selling plants is an easy way to riches. Those that try it for a living soon realise it's not so easy.

A dozen or so cabbage plants were kept for ourselves. They, along with carrots, cauliflowers, potatoes and peas, were grown in the small vegetable area of the back garden. My grandad had cared for his vegetables with great skill. I relished the challenge of continuing where he had left off. My goal was to do even better than Grandad. To achieve my targets, I had to take control.

Gardening in the 1960s was all about growing the most perfect plants possible. The back garden at Inglenook was very regimented. There was a small square lawn at the back of which I grew a double row of sweet peas and a rectangular vegetable patch behind them. A straight concrete path led down to the coal shed. The garden was enclosed by limestone walls. In front of these walls were narrow, rectangular borders. One section I devoted to herbaceous plants, one was planted with a few shrubs, and in one bed I grew chrysanthemums and in another, dahlias, with dinner plate-sized flowers. All plants, whether vegetables, flowers or shrubs, were planted in perfectly straight lines. Different kinds of plants were not allowed to mingle. Trying to create artistic compositions using different shapes, heights, textures and colours just didn't figure in those days. Oh, and it was good practice to have plenty of bare, weed-free soil around the plants.

I recently came across my *Collins Gardeners' Diary* from 1964. What a wonderful find. It contains 124 pages of gardening advice. This historic document depicts the art and science of gardening as practised fifty-six years ago.

Back then, it was all about growing perfect fruit, flowers and vegetables. Garden design wasn't mentioned.

The garden was set off by a weed-free, verdant green, manicured lawn. To achieve this horticultural utopia, the gardener had to have the killer instinct.

The diary lists a plethora of chemicals available to help the keen gardener wage war on the enemy. One notable inclusion was DDT. This was classified as an all-round insecticide in liquid or powder form. It killed anything and everything that moved. Some chemicals had an asterisk beside their names to signify that they were poisonous to animals and human beings and must be used with great care. Such lethal preparations as arsenate of lead, cyanide and nicotine were available for the amateur to buy. In hindsight, I shudder at the thought of some of the chemicals I used during the early part of my career, with little or no protective clothing for me and no regard for the natural environment.

My early diary entries for January refer to me tidying the vegetable garden and digging it over. Seed catalogues from Unwins, Dobies and Ryders (a firm long since gone) came through the letterbox this month. I spent many happy winter hours avidly reading every plant description and choosing which varieties to grow. The thrill I get from this annual experience remains undimmed.

The most significant event in the diary was on Wednesday, 25th March. Written in red biro, it simple states *Left School*. On Friday, 27th March, I pruned, sprayed and spread fertiliser around my rose trees. By Monday, 30th March, I was helping to pay my way working in the gardens of village residents.

Digging features prominently. *On Monday, dug Mr Todd's garden. On Tuesday and Wednesday, dug Mr Pighill's garden*. I have always derived a great deal of pleasure from digging. It's very satisfying to see the soil turned over deeply and evenly without a weed in sight. When a friendly robin comes up very close for a tasty worm, that feeling of being at one with nature manifests itself in a smug, self-satisfied grin.

During April, Mr Todd entrusted me to plant his potatoes and broad beans. I sowed and planted a whole range of crops in our vegetable garden. From that time onwards, I was hooked by the magic of gardens and gardening.

Six

From Apprenticeship to College

Although there were only a few horticultural employers in Westmorland, I got a job almost immediately after leaving school. To paraphrase Norman Tebbit, "I got on my bike" and cycled the 7 miles to Appleby. My destination was Banks Nurseries, owned by the Stephenson family. Father George and his three sons ran what was a general nursery business. They grew a bit of everything, including cut flowers, bedding plants, trees, shrubs and vegetables. Tom (the youngest son) managed the floristry section; Maurice (the middle son) ran the firm's shop in Appleby, and Young George (the eldest son) managed the much larger shop in Penrith.

As I pushed my bike up the hill into the nursery, my heart thumped, not with exertion, but with apprehension. Would they take me on? If so, in what capacity? I wondered.

When I got to the top, I looked around in awe. Never before had I seen such large, and so many, greenhouses. I found Maurice in one of the smaller greenhouses. He was examining and throwing out some sickly-looking cyclamen plants. The reason for their demise I would soon discover was the dreaded vine weevil.

Maurice shook my hand and gave me a warm welcome. Taking his time, he filled his Sherlock Holmes-style pipe, which he lit with one of those silver petrol lighters with a flame akin to a Bunsen burner. Once ignition was underway, the gentle questioning began.

'Now then, young man, tell me, why do you want to work in a nursery?'

I spluttered something along the lines of, 'Well, I like plants.'

'Yes, but it's hard work, in all weathers too. We can't pay you very much,' were the words which came out through clouds of St Bruno tobacco smoke. But, as I had cycled all the way from Soulby, he thought I must be keen and was prepared to offer me a three-year apprenticeship. 'You can start at the beginning of June and your wage will be £5 a week.'

I felt so ecstatic that the bike seemed to glide back home in no time at all.

Prior to starting work, I had to get some riding practice in on my dad's Vespa scooter. Since his accident, he could no longer ride it, and so he gave it to me for getting to work and back – a gift for which I was extremely grateful, even though many young men thought scooters a bit wimpish. Within a year, I had upgraded to a motorcycle. My new

David outside Inglenook 1965

steed was a BSA Bantam 175cc. A more powerful (only just) beast than the one Dad previously owned.

My first day at work wasn't quite what I expected. My foreman was a most unpleasant man in his late forties called Ernie. Ernie was a bully who tore around the nursery on a little grey Fergie. He was the original Mr Angry. He snarled at everyone, even the bosses, and didn't appear to have either a sense of humour or any patience. Not the sort of person to encourage and ease you into the world of work. How would I stand up for myself? I had no idea. I soon discovered that Ernie's irascible moods were down to too many pints of bitter every night. Mind you, he probably spent so much time in the pub to get away from his wife and seven children (six of whom were girls).

Ernie wore a cap which fitted so tightly it looked as if it was glued to his head. He never took it off and it never fell off. Everyone else knew why he never exposed his head and eventually they let me in on the secret. Ernie was bald, 100% bald – and very embarrassed by it. No one ever mentioned it to his face, because they all feared he would fly into a rage.

Despite his making my life a misery for almost three years, I learnt a great many practical skills from him in that time. If he hadn't driven me so hard then maybe I wouldn't have mastered all the basic tasks. Ernie taught me how to dig, rake, sow, plant and weed efficiently, like a professional. He instilled in me a work ethic which has never left me. As far as Ernie was concerned, gardening was all about the practical doing. Knowledge obtained from studying was coldly dismissed as mere book learning.

I was an apprentice in the era before garden centres arrived in Westmorland. Even in the more horticulturally advanced parts of the country, they were in their infancy. The rise of garden centres went hand in hand with the introduction of container-grown plants. Plants which could be sold all the year round.

At Stephenson's, sales of plants were seasonal. Bedding plants were grown in wooden seed trays. The plants were knocked out of the trays and wrapped in newspaper in dozens before going to the shops for sale. Vegetable plants were grown in the soil, lifted and wrapped in newspaper. Most trees, shrubs, roses and hedging plants had to be lifted in the dormant season as bare root plants. They were usually wrapped in hessian. The evolution of shrubs in containers was just beginning. Americans grew the first of these potted plants in large tin, catering sized jam pots.

It was this development which revolutionised the nursery industry.

Every autumn, Stephenson's imported a consignment of bare root shrubs and conifers from Holland. Ernie and I potted them into what were known as whalehide pots. Actually, they were made from strong cardboard treated with bitumen. The potted plants were labelled and set out in rows. Then the pots were covered with a mound of clinker which came from the solid fuel boilers used to heat the greenhouses. This mulch kept the weeds down and reduced moisture loss. It was a rough material to clear away by hand when it came to selecting plants for sale. The much-kinder-on-the-hands bark mulch wasn't introduced for many years. Shrubs and conifers were very popular in the mid-1960s. I learned to identify and name so many. This ability is something which stood me in good stead when I went to college, and has stayed with me over the years. Working with plants as you learn about them gives you a much deeper understanding of their needs and characteristics than simply learning from a book and reciting their names.

The plants I loved most were chrysanthemums. The nursery grew thousands, from sprays which flowered outside in August/September, to the indoor Christmas flowering large reflex (mop heads). I still grow chrysanths, and as much as I adore the flowers, it's the smell of the foliage which has always been their most endearing feature. For me, they evoke sheer nostalgia. A good whiff of their leaves and I am back as a seventeen-year-old in the nursery, planting or disbudding.

In the six weeks leading up to Christmas, we worked every day. The nursery handled 50,000-60,000 Christmas trees. They were all Norway spruce (*Picea abies*); a tree whose individual leaves wouldn't win any accolades. Groups of five, dark green, closely packed needles are arranged on upward-facing layered branches. This feature makes it ideal for festooning with baubles and lights. So-called non-needle-drop types weren't on the scene then.

The trees came in from various forests in and around the Lake District and Northumberland. A steeply sloping field led down to a road. Trees were unloaded and carried up the hill. Under Ernie's barked orders, we graded the trees for quality and size. Small ones (3-4 ft tall) were tied in bundles of five. Taller trees had their branches tied tightly to the main stem. Orders for trees came from all over the country. Lorries came daily, which we loaded and dispatched. It was very hard work and often on icy ground. Ernie never let up and he never allowed us to slacken. Towards the end of one particularly tough day, Ernie said to one of the gang, called Bob Saul (known as R Saul spoken quickly), 'What time is it when I've got time to ask?'

Bob's eyes followed him as he charged about and he dryly replied, 'Thou hasn't f***ing time.' Laughter broke out.

'Stupid bloody man,' said Ernie.

Market traders bought the second-grade trees. The slogans on their vans were memorable. Bibby's of Ingleton had on one side, *If it's good it's here,* and on the other side, *If it's here it's good.* They sold the really poor trees late in the day in fading light. The traders stood them on their toes, which they lifted a few inches to give extra height whilst turning the best side to the customers.

Maurice sometimes helped with the trees. On these occasions, he complemented his pipe with a deerstalker hat. Tom was usually too busy with floristry work. Cold snaps in winter put a spring in his step and a broad smile on his face. Cold weather meant more deaths, which in turn meant more funerals and more wreaths to make. Funerals have always been a real money-spinner for florists.

One year, my brother, John, was employed as a seasonal worker to help at Christmas tree time. For a seven-day week he got £9, not much even in those days.

Our wages were doled out as we left work on Friday afternoons. The nursery office was a green wooden building near the entrance. There was a narrow corridor behind the front door and on one side a shuttered window. Old George was paymaster general. He sat on the inside of the window. As you approached, he pulled a square brown envelope out of a little wooden box. The named envelope contained your wages. The old boy would look up at you through his good eye and in what always seemed a reluctant manner, hand over your wages. It was as if he didn't want to release his grip on your money until the very last moment.

***

Whilst doing my three-year apprenticeship at Stephenson's Nurseries, I attended horticultural day-release classes.

These classes were held at Carlisle Technical College under the auspices of the Cumberland and Westmorland College of Agriculture and Forestry. Two or three times a year, we students were treated to a visit to the farm school at Newton Rigg, where we got to do some practical work in the greenhouses and gardens.

Unlike school, I really enjoyed going to college. Somehow or other, it made sense. I was studying something I was passionate about and I couldn't learn enough. Ernie Gasgarth, however, didn't rate what he called book learning. Although he rarely ever stopped criticising me, and never praised me when I was at work, I think he missed me when I wasn't there.

After two years at college, I passed my City & Guilds exams with flying colours and was awarded 1st prize by Border Television for the best horticultural student in Cumberland, Westmorland and Dumfriesshire.

My great mentor was Henry Noblett (Ernie thought he was a cack-handed, useless know-all) who was head of the Horticultural Department at the farm school. Henry showed great faith in me and was a constant source of encouragement. After successfully completing my three-year apprenticeship at the nursery, I left Stephenson's and became a full-time student at Carlisle Technical College. This decision was based entirely on Henry's recommendation. He had constantly pointed out that unless I got some decent qualifications, I was likely to remain a lowly paid gardener for the rest of my working life. This, he insisted, would be a dreadful waste of my ability.

The first step would be to get sufficient GCE/ O-levels to gain acceptance as a full-time student at one of the top agricultural colleges in the country. Carlisle Technical College was to be the first rung on the ladder of my climb up the horticultural world. A few words of praise for pointing me in the right direction should also go to Laurie Walker. Now, Laurie worked at Stephenson's as a foreman. I only spent short periods working with him and his wife, but oh what a contrasting character to Ernie. For a start, he was a teetotal Methodist lay preacher; even so, he was a pretty normal okay sort of bloke who gave me lots of encouragement. One day, I was potting up some *Primula obconicas*. Laurie's face instantly became swollen if he touched his skin with the sap of this plant. As he watched me, he said that if I was determined enough, I could end up with Henry Noblett's job one day. Many years down the line, this came to pass, but more about that later.

Upon Henry's recommendation and his willingness to act as my referee, I applied to become a full-time student at Writtle Agricultural College near Chelmsford. Now, Henry's advice had always stood me in good stead, but Essex was the other end of the country, for goodness' sake! – near London and reputedly as flat as a pancake. All this to a Westmorland lad who had strayed outside of his home county on no more than half a dozen occasions, was a pretty scary prospect. Still, I felt that at twenty years of age, it was time to take this giant leap forward into the unknown. The thought of spending the rest of my life in Soulby spurred me on to put pen to paper and fill in the application form.

In the autumn of 1968, I received a letter asking me to attend for interview at Writtle. After a long train journey, I was met at Chelmsford Railway Station by a Mr Harry Baker, a small grey-haired man with what, to me, was a very funny accent (Kentish, I was later to learn). Mr Baker turned out to be a horticultural technician who had been despatched by the vice principal to collect me from the station and give me a guided tour of the college prior to my interview.

The facilities at Writtle totally blew my mind. I had never seen horticulture on this scale before. The orchards, which stretched for mile upon mile, contained trees whose branches were laden down almost to the point of breaking with the most colourful mouth-watering apples and pears. The glasshouse complex seemed immense as it shimmered like a vast lake in the strong Essex sunlight. What did they do with all those chrysanthemums, carnations, roses, tomatoes, cucumbers and lettuces? I wondered, not daring to ask in case I came across as a northern simpleton. The gardens around the college buildings were no less inspiring, containing a whole host of plants I had never seen before. It was, however, quite reassuring to be able to recognise a lot of the hardy plants. A testament to my time at Banks Nurseries and to Henry's fine teaching.

Following the tour and a meal, I felt butterflies in my stomach as interview time approached. My fears were well founded, for at mid-afternoon I was ushered into the vice principal's office. A tall, distinguished gentleman with thickset jowls and grey receding hair indicated to me to sit down. His long fingers pointed to a chair at the far end of his office. I meekly sat down and felt very intimidated. I was grilled for what seemed like hours by Mr Healey (later I found out his first name was Austin, at least his parents had a sense of humour – he certainly didn't).

After asking all the typical questions, including: 'Why did you apply to Writtle?' 'Do you think you will be able to cope with the demands of the course?' 'How easy will it be for you to settle in Essex?' and so on and so forth, Mr Healey ended the interview very abruptly and simply said he would be in touch. This to me felt like a rejection. Oh yes, in the '60s and '70s, entry onto a course wasn't just about having the minimum entry requirements. Colleges and universities were able to select; it wasn't just about bums on seats. As a twenty-year-old today, I could get onto almost any course if I were able to demonstrate that I could benefit. Many would say that if you can pass the steaming-the-mirror test, you're in.

Several weeks went by and I had given up all hope of getting into Writtle when a letter dropped through the letterbox. I could see by the Chelmsford postmark that this could only mean one thing. Was it Yes or No? Shaking like a leaf, I ripped it open. The first time I read the letter, I was stunned. I couldn't believe it. The second time, it sunk in. Yes, I had been accepted on the Ordinary National Diploma Course at Writtle Agricultural College and was to start in September 1969.

Seven

A Giant Step for a Country Boy

Neil Armstrong set foot on the moon on 11th July 1969. Two months later, an equally momentous event took place in my life. I left home for college.

My grey mini van was given all the last-minute checks. Tyres, water, windscreen washers and oil level – all correct. Finally, the petrol tank was filled to capacity. My dad's old-style suitcase (brown, with a buckled strap over the middle to stop it bursting open) bulged with clothes. Mam had sown name tags to everything, even socks. My parents waved me off in the early hours. The last thing Mam said was, 'Ring home as soon as you get there.'

I studied the *AA Book of the Road* meticulously and wrote down every stage of the 260-mile journey. It was a six-hour journey. Fifty years ago, roads were narrower and twisted through many small towns and villages. Now there are motorways, dual carriageways and bypasses. Today, there are faster vehicles and faster roads, yet it still takes six hours. Considerably longer if roadworks or accidents cause delays. I often think that if aliens are looking down on us they must think we are bonkers as we cover an ever greater percentage of ground with roads to accommodate our mobile tin boxes.

As I entered the college drive, my nerves grabbed me like a fish hook. I had come all this way and couldn't back out now. Suddenly this new world which I had yearned for seemed scary. All my familiar surroundings, family and friends were at the other end of the country. I wouldn't see them for fourteen weeks.

Come on, don't be pathetic, I told myself. *You wanted to go to college and get away from the restrictive confines of Soulby.* So I parked the van and followed the signs telling new students where to report. Once inside the building, I spotted a public telephone. After a brief call home to put my parents' minds at rest, I reported at the arrivals desk. Most of the other new students looked as nervous as I felt.

After the initial checking-in, we had to enrol on the course we were to study. Mine was an Ordinary National Diploma in Amenity Horticulture. This was to be the first year ever for this course. I was one of the guinea pigs – one of thirty.

I don't remember most of what happened on the rest of that first day. We were shown the dining room and told when mealtimes were. Next morning, we had to report to a particular room at nine o'clock. Everyone was given a room key and pointed in the direction of their rooms. The building which was to be my home was called Gill Hostel. It was a single-storey, red brick building. After unpacking, I sat on the bed and stared at the cramped little room in a state of bemused fear.

Lots of noisy chattering came down the corridor. There were accents I had never heard before. Eventually, I plucked up enough courage to see where it came from. The common room near the front entrance was packed. I went in and merged into the background. I soon learned there were boys from Norfolk, Northern Ireland, Kent, Surrey, Yorkshire and Malta. Where on earth is Malta? I thought, but was too shy to ask.

A tallish, angular lad with swept-back sandy coloured hair ambled across to me. 'You look like a rabbit caught in a car's headlights,' were his first words.

'Well, I do feel a bit dazed.'

'So where do you come from? Somewhere up north?' he said.

'Westmorland. It's above Yorkshire and before Cumberland. Do you know it?'

'Aye, I do that. By the way, my name's John, John Fryer from Leeds and that's in Yorkshire, God's own country. What's thy name?'

'It's David, David Haigh. My dad was born in Leeds.'

Soon we met another newcomer from Yorkshire called Melvyn Crooks, from Sheffield. Being one of a newly formed trio of northerners was a giant boost to my confidence at the end of my first day.

Other memorable characters included the very tall blond-haired David French. He took his studies very seriously. For him, life was a sombre affair. Some of us were given nicknames. I got off lightly as mine was Ingle – shortened version of Inglenook. Roger Mellors was known as Stinky Smellers, just because it rhymed. Mary Smee was cruelly called Hairy Knee. It wasn't long before Fryer became known as Mumbles due to his low-volume, incomprehensible Yorkshire accent.

***

'Right, chaps, follow me,' barked Mr Clarke. He seemed to be unaware of the fact that there were two girls in the group. He strode off and we all tried to keep pace with the immaculately turned out lecturer. His shiny brogues reflected the leaves from the tree under which he had assembled his charges. The "Major", as he was soon christened, had a slender, upright body, closely cropped black hair and a hint of mischief in his twinkly eyes. 'In his early thirties,' was the opinion of a few of the course members.

Once inside the orchard, he gave us reams of facts about the types of fruit grown and how many acres of each. I remember there being around 60 acres in total. I had never seen fruit of this scale or of this quantity or quality. Orchards in Westmorland consisted of a few trees in a small paddock. In comparison, crops were small and quality mediocre. I soon learned that this was due to deep, high-grade soils, less rainfall, more sunlight and higher light levels in East Anglia.

The Major seemed to have 360-degree vision. If anybody's hand went anywhere near a tasty apple or pear, he bellowed out his awareness of this misdemeanour with the words, 'Don't even think about it, boy.'

Our first trip around the orchards finished at the fruit store. This was a large concrete building. Inside were temperature-, humidity- and CO_2-controlled rooms big enough to accommodate a forklift truck. Apples and pears were stored in large wooden crates for several months.

The fruit store was also used for practical classes. The following March, the Major was teaching us how to graft fruit trees. Grafting is a type of highly skilled horticultural carpentry which enables different varieties of fruit to be grown on the most suitable root systems. The end result is bigger crops of better quality fruit, produced on trees of a more manageable size.

We all had to practise what we had been shown. My attempt was a disaster. The knife slipped and went into my finger. I caught sight of the bone and fell to the concrete floor, losing consciousness. I came round in an instant, my finger stinging like fury. Mr Clarke had instructed the technician to pour iodine over the wound.

'Okay, Clive, stick a plaster on that cut and take him to hospital.'

'Yes, Mr Clarke, will do,' replied his assistant.

No stitches were needed, but I can still see the mark left by the knife. I have never been able to cope with the sight of blood without fainting since that day.

Despite this experience, I always enjoyed learning about fruit whilst at college. Growing fruit is a most rewarding aspect of gardening which has always given me great satisfaction.

The secrets behind the college's perfect fruit were revealed over the years. Correct pruning and nutrition played their part. However, it was the frequent use of insecticides and fungicides to control pests and diseases which were largely responsible. Every ten days without fail, from bud-break to leaf-fall, a tractor and sprayer loaded with a cocktail of potent chemicals went up and down the orchard rows. Any creature which moved, either harmful or beneficial, was killed. Prevention not cure was normal commercial practice in the late 1960s and early 1970s.

Bert Davies was a highly regarded fruit lecturer. He was a softly spoken, gentle man in his late fifties, very distinguished-looking, with wavy, swept-back silver hair and silver spectacles. Mr Davies loved his apples. Every lecture was devoted to apples. He never got round to the other fruits that were on the syllabus. The most memorable thing he told us was about his honeymoon which had to be cut to a couple of days. It was, as he told us, "nicotine time and the trees had to be sprayed". This revelation caused great mirth in the class, but poor old Bert couldn't understand why.

***

Visits to places of horticultural interest were an integral part of the course. They were enjoyed by all students. It was a day away from the lecture room and a chance to see other parts of East Anglia.

The first-ever visit was as I well remember the most boring. We went to Harlow (Harlow New Town) as it was called. Harlow was created in 1947, which makes it the same age as me. It was one of several new towns built to house the overspill from London. Harlow was built for 60,000 people and designed by the architect Frederick Gibberd. It lays claim to two firsts – the first-ever all-pedestrian shopping precinct and the first residential tower block. Our reason to visit this soulless modern development was to marvel at the landscaping. Nothing worth remembering has stuck in my mind.

However, it does bring back memories of the lecturer responsible for this trip. Barry Potter had recently graduated and was very green. He took a lot of ribbing and worse from the students. Being the owner of a green Reliant Robin, that wasn't surprising. A group of students whom he had upset in some way decided they would teach the cocky upstart a well-deserved lesson. There was a small but deep lake in the college grounds. I think it was a reservoir for supplying water to the orchards. The boys made a wooden raft. They then fastened Potter's three-wheeler on top before floating it out into the centre of the lake. Everyone but Barry thought it a great joke. Mr Potter got his car back after a couple of days. It was undamaged. I don't think the offenders were ever identified.

For me, the most memorable and useful visits were to nurseries. Tony Clarke had transferred from the orchards to the hardy nursery stock section (tree and shrub) production. He put on many excellent trips.

Blooms of Bressingham near Diss in Norfolk proved to be a great day out. It was very entertaining as well as educational. This famous nursery was started by the late Alan Bloom. He was responsible for introducing somewhere in the region of 200 new kinds of perennials. The nursery beds were on a grand scale – very orderly and weed-free with young plants of the highest quality. Alan was developing the Dell Garden next to Bressingham Hall to showcase not only his plants but his novel way of growing them in island beds surrounded by lawns.

His other great passion was steam engines. He built a narrow gauge track around the nursery. We students all cheered when we saw him driving his engine. Dressed in oily black clothes with his straight, long white hair almost down to his backside, he blew the whistle in acknowledgement as he passed in a cloud of steam.

The visit to the Beth Chatto Gardens and nursery at Elmstead Market near Colchester was another fantastic day. For one student, it nearly didn't happen. My mate Nigel Goodall was about to get on the bus when the Major bawled him out. 'Goodall, what's that on your head?' he yelled.

'It's a hat, Mr Clarke,' said Nigel. (It was a multi-coloured woollen bobble hat.)

Such attire was unacceptable in 1969. With his lips curling and nose twitching with anger, the military-style lecturer roared, 'Don't be impudent, boy. Get rid of it or you don't get on the bus. This college has high standards to maintain.' The hat was removed and off we went.

The Beth Chatto Gardens were begun in 1960 and the nursery had only just been opened. Beth Chatto was in her mid-forties. She welcomed the course and took us round. Her enthusiasm, knowledge and desire to create a spectacular garden on such an unpromising site was inspirational. Tony Clarke appeared most enamoured by her.

'She's dynamite, chaps, don't you think?' he beamed as we boarded the bus back to Writtle.

***

The Ordinary National Diploma wasn't the most demanding course. Just as well, because more time was spent on extra-mural activities than studying.

Visits to the nearest pub were a regular event in my first year at college. Myself, John Fryer and Melvyn Crookes drank at the Wheatsheaf almost every night. A short walk from college, it was a tiny pub with one narrow bar. The landlady and landlord, called Janet and John, made students very welcome, unlike the pub on the other side of the road whose name I can't remember.

I wasn't a connoisseur of beer, having little experience of the different brands at the time. Fryer being your boastful Yorkshireman claimed he knew everything about ale. He insisted it should have a frothy head. The Wheatsheaf's ale didn't have any froth. It was real ale. It was kept in wooden barrels behind the bar. It was a local beer made by a small local brewery – Grays of Chelmsford. Our taste buds soon developed a real liking for a pint of Grays' bitter.

I was inducted into the dominos game of 5s and 3s. Success depended to a great extent on which dominoes you held. There wasn't much skill involved. We often played dominoes with Rosie from the village. At the time, she seemed very old, but was probably only in her fifties. What was certain was the copious number of barley wines she could drink, especially if she persuaded others to buy them for her. Invariably, in her intoxicated state, she would break into song – always it was *Roll Me Over*, a bawdy little number, but harmless enough.

Most nights, we played darts. Never being good at mental arithmetic, I tried to avoid my turn at keeping score. Mind you – my scores were usually fairly low. Fryer was a decent player and never failed to let us know. One night, however, a scary incident shook him out of his bragging. The dartboard was just to one side of the entrance door. Up stepped John with his customary swagger. 'Double top for the game. Here goes then,' he announced. As he released the first dart, the door opened and in walked a middle-aged lady. The dart hit the outside wire of the board and flew towards her face. It skimmed past her left eye, touching the skin on its way. The woman was hysterical and her husband went ballistic, Fryer was very apologetic. But neither husband or wife would be placated. The landlord offered free drinks which took the sting out of the situation. We never finished the game, thinking it was best to make a hasty retreat back to college.

Wednesday afternoons were free from lectures. Students could choose how they spent this time, including doing nothing. There were various clubs you could join, such as Music and Photography. Playing sport was by far the most popular. I chose football. My college career got off to a sorry start. I didn't even get to the pitch. Without warming up, I began to run towards the sports field. After a few yards, I came to a sudden excruciatingly painful stop. Barely able to move, I made my sorry way to the doctor's surgery just up the road. Doctor Graves was the college doctor.

The doctor was in his early fifties, of medium build with greying hair and wearing gold-rimmed spectacles. 'You've pulled a thigh muscle,' was his instant diagnosis. 'It will be very sore for some time. No vigorous exercise until it heals.'

When I did get fit, I was picked for the college team. I played on the right wing. Being short on the skill front, I made up for it with my single-minded obsession with scoring goals. I scored a few, including a hat trick in one memorable match against the local police. My marker was a loud-mouthed, obnoxious thug of a man who tried to intimidate me with threats to break my legs. I was terrified every time the ball was passed to me. The increasingly loud thud of his boots as he pounded closer to me meant I was scared witless. Every time I aimed for goal before the hulk got anywhere near me. The cards must have fallen kindly for me. We won the game by 5 goals to 3. I scored three goals and to my relief finished the match unscathed.

Twenty-five years later, soon after meeting my second wife, Barbara, she told me that one of her best friends, Jane, was the daughter of Dr Graves. Jane grew up at the surgery in Writtle. Barbara hails from Great Dunmow in Essex and they both went to art college in Colchester. They both spent a lot of time together in Writtle around this period. Quite amazingly, our paths never crossed.

Frustratingly, I made no progress with the opposite sex during my first year at college. My shyness was the biggest hurdle. Additionally, the low percentage of female students drastically reduced the odds. I was friendly with one of the two girls on our course. Kate Mcinerny had shoulder-length coal black hair and dusky skin. She was mostly of Portuguese descent. We went on a day trip together to Westonbirt Arboretum in Gloucestershire. The trees and shrubs were stunning and majestic. However, they weren't uppermost in my thoughts. The same evening, we went to the cinema and saw Clint Eastwood in *Play Misty for Me*. When we got back to Kate's mini, a window had been smashed and her expensive camera stolen. The theft left her so distressed that all thoughts of intimacy were shattered like the window.

By the third term, I had formed new friendships. Nigel Goodall was from Stoke-on-Trent. Of stocky build, black hair and thick-rimmed glasses, Nige had a dry sense of humour. He had a record player and probably the best record collection in college at that time, which enhanced his popularity. Like many other students, his records introduced me to the likes of the Eagles, Rod Stewart, Elton John, Carole King and Van Morrison.

Goodall was friends with Pete Ramsey from Guildford. They both owned Austin Champs (similar to American Jeeps). When starting up, the engines growled like angry lions which had been woken too soon whilst still digesting their last kill. A lot of time was devoted to tinkering with these open-topped vehicles. It was great fun to mess about with these lads and to drink with them. Despite this lack of application, we all got through our first year without breaking sweat.

Eight

A Capital Twelve Months
at Kew Gardens

Decimal currency was introduced in Britain. The average price of a house was £5,000. Greenpeace was born. I was spending twelve months at the Royal Botanic Gardens, Kew. It was part of my three-year diploma course. Students were given the chance to suggest where they would like to spend this time of practical training.

Pete Ramsay and I opted for Kew. Why not aim high? *It's worth a shot* was our thinking. For Pete, who hailed from Guildford, it wasn't far from home. I had never been to London. The possibility of learning at the world-famous Kew Gardens was a prospect I couldn't contemplate when I left school. To our amazement, strings were pulled by Mr Sales our course manager, and Kew accepted us.

It was 1971 and I was flat-sharing in Chiswick. Number 52 Barrowgate Road was a large Victorian house on three levels. The most famous resident on the street was Tommy Cooper. Tommy was often seen in the Queen's Head. His massive frame and craggy features were a source of great amusement before he even opened his mouth. You could never get near him. Fans, or hangers-on, probably some of both, swarmed around him.

We shared our accommodation with a few of Pete's friends. Hughie and his girlfriend Fiona were there shortly before we moved in. Hughie was a grey man with closely cropped grey hair. He was a few years older than us. Every morning, immaculately groomed and wearing his grey pinstriped suit, he trudged off to his boring office job with Shell. His evenings were spent in his room with his mousey wife-to-be. They moved out fairly soon after our arrival. His replacement, Peter Graham Robert Williamson, otherwise known as Pod or Fat Boy (out of earshot) was training to be something high up in the wine trade. A perk of his job was being given a few bottles of wine which hadn't passed muster in the tasting tests. About once a week, Pod's briefcase would be bulging with cast-offs. With a few exceptions, we found them perfectly quaffable. He was a useful extrovert character to share with.

Not so Steve. He contributed virtually nothing. He didn't work. I don't know where his share of the rent came from. He had soft, milky skin, floppy blond hair and flabby lips. His appearance and voice were most effeminate. I don't think he was too keen on me, either. In his view, I was just a basic northerner. His ambition was to be a DJ on the pirate station, Radio London. He spent weeks putting together a demo tape. Within days of him finally submitting his passport to fame on the airwaves, the government took the station off air. Steve moped around for weeks bemoaning his bad luck. I did feel sorry for him, but only for a short time. There was no shortage of jobs at that time, yet he didn't try to find work.

Pete and I shared transport to Kew. I still had my mini-van, which I upgraded to a mini saloon. Minis were one of the most popular cars on the road. The flamboyant Pete, with his flowing locks of dark brown hair, had an open-topped Austin Champ. This vehicle was the equivalent of the American Jeep. They were widely deployed during World War II. You never went unnoticed in his vehicle. We were often running late. Tea and toast would be consumed as we navigated the roundabout under Chiswick Flyover. Dangerous manoeuvres, especially for the driver.

Not as dangerous as riding under the flyover on a tandem in the early hours of the morning. Such stupidity came at the end of a party when much alcohol had been consumed. A persuasive blonde girl called Lorraine convinced (it didn't take much) me to pedal with her to Heathrow Airport. She said it would be brilliant to watch the jumbo jets take off and land. Jumbos were still novel and exciting to see.

I was in such a nervous tizzy on my first day at Kew. We entered the gardens through the main gate. The admission charge was one old penny. It now costs £17.50 for an adult and for a young person (aged 16-24) the ticket price is £9. We didn't have to pay, but were told to stay at the gate until one of the curators met us. Mr Brown was in his fifties with a West Country burr. When he shook hands, his coarse, soil-stained fingers exuded practical experience. He put us at ease and told us which departments we were to work in for the first three months. I was put into the tree and shrub sector and Pete was to work with alpines. We each went off with a supervisor for an introductory tour.

I was staggered by the phenomenal number of plants. Every plant had a label and every label contained a mine of information. Which plant family it belonged to, its botanical name, the year it was planted and which country it originated from. So many plants, from so many places. So much to absorb, and only twelve months to do it in.

***

Jets rumbled overhead. One every minute. We were on the flight path to Heathrow Airport. In complete contrast, autumn leaves fell silently like tiny parachutes jostling for position in a crowded sky. They came from the thousands of exotic trees and shrubs imported from all over the world a century ago. The ground was soon covered in a glorious carpet of yellow, orange and red. If left where they fell, the grass would go yellow. This couldn't be allowed to happen at the Royal Botanic Gardens, Kew. All the leaves had to be collected and turned into compost. This job had to be repeated until all the trees were leafless.

In the autumn of 1970, Eddie and I raked leaves for five weeks. He was a young Canadian with broad shoulders and strong, angular facial features. His mental tenacity was as strong as his physical strength. He was an inspiration. With his mindset, no job was boring or tedious. During the first day, I hardly spoke; only grunted if I had to.

During the afternoon tea break, Eddie broke my silence. 'Why have you got a face like a cat's arse?'

'Because I don't fancy doing this for weeks. Thought I came here to learn, not be cheap labour.'

Eddie introduced the idea of identifying trees and shrubs by their leaf shapes and dormant skeletons. 'Use this time to look closely at the characteristics of the bark, the outline of their branches and the differences between the twigs and the buds. Don't waste your time grumbling about the job. Take advantage of all the plants we encounter, many of which you will not see anywhere else but here at Kew.' Wise words from this affable twenty-four-year-old.

With an 'Oh, all right. I suppose it's worth a go,' I picked up my rake again.

It wasn't long before we added a competitive edge to our daily task. We challenged each other with twigs and leaves. A kind of "name that plant" competition. Thanks to Eddie, this seemingly thankless task turned into a fun-loving learning experience.

Every autumn since those days, when the leaves come falling down, my thoughts turn to foliage-related memories. For nineteen years up to 2019, Knowefield Wood, Carlisle, was a two-minute walk from our front door. This small block of trees is the last remnant of a tree and shrub nursery which covered 400 acres. The leafy carpet over which I trod each autumn was dominated by *Acer platanoides* (Norway maple). Its large, rich yellow, five-lobed leaves resemble those of a plane tree. It's reassuring to know that this tree was introduced into the UK in the 17th century. That's 400 years before I was born. How many offspring have been produced in four centuries? I have known this species and its cultivars since my days as an apprentice at Stephensons' Nurseries in Appleby.

Ron Rule, our supervisor at Kew, cycled around the gardens visiting the staff under his control. We saw him twice a day. A dapper chap in his late thirties, Ron always approached us on his green ladies bike with a friendly smile. A couple of days before the end of the leaf-sweeping season, he told us he was impressed by our teamwork and he'd chosen us for a rather special job. 'I want you to be responsible for lifting all the viburnums in the gardens and relocating them. Kew is going to establish the National Collection of Viburnums.'

Nowadays, plants in a collection are normally interspersed with those of other genera in mixed borders to create an aesthetically pleasing design. Back in 1970, a collection of a particular genus was given a designated section of the garden. All the species, cultivars and varieties were grown in one area. Ron wanted us to collect all the different types of viburnum and replant them in a large border by the side of the Orangery. Eddie and I were delighted to be chosen for this prestigious task. The grins on our faces were wider than Kew Bridge. Putting his bike clips round the bottom of his green waterproof trousers, Ron in his quiet manner asked, 'You're happy with that, are you?' He didn't need an answer, nor waited for one, as he rode off down the Broad Walk. This wide tarmacked drive leading to the Palm House was flanked by an avenue of tulip trees. They were all brought down by the Great Storm on 15th October 1987.

It took about six weeks to complete the job. I recorded every day, every plant and where it came from, and its position on a plan of the new collection in my college diary. The diary was to be assessed when I returned to Writtle at the start of my third year. Sadly and foolishly, I long since got rid of my diary. A wealth of information and memories gone. Fortunately not all forgotten.

***

Wakehurst Place is a satellite garden under the management of Kew. On a sunny summer's day in 1971, Eddie and I, together with two of Eddie's female friends (Sandra and Louise), took a day trip to Wakehurst.

We all loved the gardens. The attractive layout blended effortlessly into the gently rolling Sussex countryside. Wakehurst looked and felt as if it had benefitted from the guiding hand of an artist, whereas Kew with its many formally laid-out collections came over as mainly the work of a scientist.

After an enjoyable morning, Sandra came up with a plan for the afternoon. 'Why don't we go to the Church of Scientology? I know the back way in so we won't have to pay.' All I knew was that it was some kind of religious group. I didn't like the idea of visiting, especially sneaking in a back entrance without paying. The others were all for it.

"Come on. It will be a laugh," said Eddie.

As we entered the wooded grounds, a large modern building appeared between the trees in the near distance. We nervously walked from the back of the house to the front steps. At the top was a pair of heavy wooden doors. Eddie was about to ring the bell when a side door creaked open. A suave-looking man in his early thirties with slicked-back, unnaturally black hair and horn-rimmed glasses greeted us. In a drawling American accent, he uttered the words, 'Do come in. You're most welcome.' He looked and sounded the epitome of insincerity.

Larry gave us a guided tour of the rooms he wanted us to see. Portraits of the founder L. Ron Hubbard looked down on us from every wall. Of course, we were told how this wonderful benefactor had financed the Church of Scientology. All that was asked of us was that we keep an open mind – there would be no pressure on us to join. Finally, we went into a room filled with Heath Robinson-style equipment. One contraption could tell if our minds were confused and anxious or calm and at ease.

The equipment consisted of two baked bean-sized cans which were wired up to a meter – a bit like a swingometer. You had to hold a can in each hand and when Larry flicked a switch, the needle would swing left for calm and right for anxious. I reasoned that if the cans were gripped tightly, the needle would swing violently to the right. When my turn came, I kept a loose grip and came out as well adjusted.

The message was clear enough. If you fell for their brainwashing and your mind was disturbed, then the Church of Scientology would be your saviour – provided you signed up and agreed to pay for your salvation. None of us were that gullible.

We thanked Larry for a most enlightening experience. Then we made a hasty retreat out of the confines of this mind-manipulating sect and back inside the safety of Louise's car.

Returning to London, we reflected on the day's events. We all agreed that Wakehurst warranted a full day's visit if we ever returned. But the Church of Scientology and the creepy Larry would never see us again.

***

I was paid £20 a week whilst at Kew. In order to supplement my wages, I volunteered for weekend duty in the Palm House. Built between 1844 and 1848, the Palm House is Kew's most recognisable building – an iconic Victorian glass and iron structure. The conditions created inside are to replicate a tropical rainforest. It was extremely hot. A tiring environment in which to spend an eight-hour working day.

Weekend duty involved two gardeners watering, picking up fallen leaves and generally keeping the place immaculate. You also had to try to answer visitors' questions or point them in the direction of someone who could. You were expected to be helpful and courteous at all times. On one occasion, I fell from these high standards. It was closing time, 6 pm on Sunday. We were worn out and ready for home. We rang the bell five minutes before time and walked through the Palm House, letting the public know we were about to close. Fifteen minutes later and voices could still be heard. Clearly, one particular family was making sure it got its money's worth.

It was then that I had a devious plan. 'Why don't we turn on the automatic overhead irrigation?'

Brian, my work mate, was flabbergasted. 'Hell – no, you can't do that!'

'Too late now,' I said, grinning as I pulled down the lever which started the electric motor. Within seconds, there was much screaming and cursing as the unwanted guests scurried towards the exit.

A few days later, Charlie Erskine, the curator, responsible for the Palm House, called me into his office to inform me he had received a complaint from a member of the public regarding a visit with his wife and two children to the gardens. The incident in question involved them getting soaked when they visited the Palm House. With plum-coloured embarrassment rising up through my face, I stuttered to explain my frustration when the visitors refused to leave. 'I told them we were closing at least twice, but they took no notice.'

Mr Erskine tried his best to come over as a strict disciplinarian, but his nature betrayed him. In his refined Scottish accent, all he could muster was, 'You will have to be a wee bit more diplomatic, David, when dealing with the public.'

***

Sam was a short, slim Scotsman with a narrow face and a full head of wiry, grey hair. He was the supervisor of the tree gang. This gang of four maintained all the trees at Kew. Any which were deemed dangerous, they felled. It was my good fortune to work with them for six weeks.

Big Tom and Little Tom were two West Indians who did most of the pruning. At about five and a half feet tall, Little Tom never left the ground. His job was to collect all the prunings and stack them prior to disposal. He was such a jovial little man, always smiling and singing reggae tunes. His bright eyes were magnetic focal points in his round face.

Big Tom was about fifteen years older. He went about his tasks in a languid fashion. Carrying his long-handled pruning saw, Tom the elder placed his ladder against the tree which needed pruning. As he ascended, the gentle giant surveyed the entire tree. He was looking for a suitable fork in the branches in which to position his 6-ft tall frame. Once settled, he made sure his dark brown trilby was nestled firmly on his big, broad head. Any branches and small limbs which needed to be removed were done so effortlessly by Tom and his razor-sharp saw. He only came down from the trees at breaktimes. He said very little and smiled even less.

The two Toms fried fish every lunchtime. I don't think the frying pan was ever cleaned. The pungent, unpleasant smell pervaded the air some distance from the mess room. The thought of it takes me back more than fifty years.

Mickey, the fourth member of the team, was a Londoner in his mid-twenties. A spiv-like character, he could always lay his hands on anything for half the amount you had paid for it. He was a qualified arboriculturalist trained in the safe use of chainsaws and the latest tree surgery and tree-climbing techniques. Under his instruction, I learned to ascend and descend trees safely. But, like Little Tom, I felt uneasy when my feet left the ground. I was always nervous near chainsaws, and the combination of wielding one of these noisy, dangerous machines 30 feet up a tree wasn't the kind of plant care I wanted to be involved in.

Many of Kew's old and rare trees catalogued the changes which had taken place in tree surgery techniques. Several of these venerable specimens were part concrete. Cavities and hollows in the trunks and branches had been filled with this unyielding material in the preceding decades. It had been thought that concrete would strengthen the trees, stop further rot and therefore extend the trees' lives. As time passed, this practice was found to cause more damage to the trees. Injury occurs when a tree continues to move in the wind against the stiff concrete inside. The resulting abrasion allows decay to move into the living wood.

By the early 1970s, concrete had given way to the technique of clearing hollows of rotten organic matter and decaying wood. Mickey was fully conversant with the latest methods. Most importantly, he was delighted to show me these modern ways and encourage me to help him. The insides of cavities were treated with a preserving paint which was thought at the time would prevent fungal spores entering the wood. Fine wire mesh was fastened on the top of the holes to stop leaves and other debris falling in and becoming trapped in the bottom. A hole was drilled in the bottom of the cavity and a downward-sloping plastic pipe inserted to drain away the moisture.

On one memorable winter's day, a fierce gale made it too dangerous to climb trees or even work under them. Sam, Mickey and I were in the tool shed catching up on the maintenance of equipment. It was a tranquil scene. We were just pottering around between cups of tea. Every thirty minutes or so, Mickey stopped work, sat on an upturned wooden crate, got out his packet of Golden Virginia and his red Rizla cigarette papers, made a roll-up and lit it with his petrol lighter.

Bliss was shattered by a reverberating crack which seemed to last for ages. 'What the f**k was that, Sam?' said a visibly shaken Mickey.

'A tree has come down on the island, that's my guess. It's happened before. We'll go out tomorrow in the boat, weather permitting.'

Next day, we packed ropes, hand saws and a chainsaw into the small boat, and Sam rowed us the short distance to the small island. As we approached, we knew Sam was right. A 60-ft tall *Taxodium distichum* (swamp cypress) had snapped off about 20 ft from ground level. It had fallen towards the water. As it crashed down, the trunk had become caught in the limbs of several nearby trees. Collateral damage was extensive. Once on land, Sam surveyed the wreckage and huffed, 'Might have known. Bloody woodpeckers again,' whilst pointing out the holes their beaks had made.

***

From the tree gang, I moved to the tree and shrub nursery. Although only about 1 hectare in size, the nursery was home to a variety of activities.

Most of the ground was devoted to rows of young trees and shrubs. These plants were being grown in the ground prior to planting in the final positions in the gardens. The soil in which they grew was mulched to retain moisture and to reduce weed growth. For this purpose, spent hops, a by-product of the brewing industry, were provided free of charge by Young's – a local brewery. Their hoppy aroma lingered long and sweet.

Not a plant in the nursery was out of line. Military style rows ran from north to south. Maintenance was immaculate. That was until I was given the job of planting out fifty small heathers. As I finished the task, I was quite proud of my work. Charlie Erskine soon deflated my ego. Yes, he was the curator who had to take me to task for soaking a family of visitors to the Palm House. 'That's not a very tidy job, is it, David? You haven't raked the soil level before you put the plants in, have you?'

'It will be fine once the plants grow and cover the soil,' I replied.

'That's like saying everything looks the same when it's covered in snow,' he retorted. He was telling me to always work to the highest professional standards. That lesson stayed with me throughout my career.

A more painful lesson soon followed. I parked my mini-van in a side street opposite one of the minor entrances into Kew Gardens. Something I had done many times before in the summer of 1971. This morning turned out to be very different.

As I walked towards the gate, I spotted a tall girl, with blonde hair halfway down her back, on the opposite side of the road. She was extremely beautiful, her figure perfect. As I walked, I looked, no, stared in wonder and lust. She never gave me a glance. Still I gawped at her. From nowhere, I was dealt an almighty blow. I had walked into a concrete lamppost. My forehead came off second in this confrontation. My raging hormones were put instantly in their place. Feeling queasy, I went through the gate, past the gatekeeper, who said, 'Good morning, young man,' without looking up.

Five minutes later, I walked into the nursery mess room. Two of the other gardeners were about to go out and start work. As they got up from their seats, they stopped and stared at me. 'What's happened to you? That looks really nasty,' said Alan.

I put my hand on my forehead, felt a massive lump, wobbled and sat down, feeling dizzy and sick. 'God, you look bad. Let's get you to hospital,' said Tom.

At Richmond Hospital, they cleaned up my head. The damage was superficial. I was told the swelling would go down in a few days. The bruise would be a reminder of my foolish actions for considerably longer. I was to go home and rest for the day. But, before I left, I was to have a tetanus injection. A staff nurse would attend to me soon.

Before long, my name was called by a sturdy, grey-haired nurse dressed in a blue and grey uniform. Her face looked as if it couldn't smile. Her skin was so tightly stretched it didn't appear to have any elasticity. She issued her orders with a foreign tongue. I had no evidence to support my theory, but I took her to be Greek. Inside her room, she told me to take down my trousers and lie face down on the bed. Without warning, she yanked down my underpants and thrust what felt like a large nail into my right buttock. 'Okay, pull up your trousers. You can go now,' were her brusque final instructions.

The nursery had a small greenhouse section. It acted as the nursery for tender plants. When these babies got large enough, they would be transferred to larger greenhouses such as the Palm House and the Temperate House. There they took their place in the limelight. They would be in the public domain and had to leave the nursery in peak condition. Bert the foreman carried out a routine spraying programme against pest and disease attack. Kew was at the forefront when it came to health and safety issues. Bert looked every part the astronaut in his protective clothing; knapsack sprayer on his back. He was a mild-mannered old boy with a broad West Country accent. Somewhat of a weather guru, he would often greet you with an update on his barometer readings. 'Barometers rising. Good spell ahead, warm and sunny for the next few days, I shouldn't wonder,' was one of his favourite lines.

The "Seed Bank" was a small red brick building in the bottom left-hand corner of the nursery. My last three weeks at Kew were spent in this building. Seeds of all the specimens collected by Kew's plant hunters found their way here. Most of my time was spent sieving out all the chaff and debris. The seeds were then passed on to senior technicians who labelled all the different seeds. Information on the seeds contained the family, genus and species. When, where and the name of the collector responsible was also logged. The seeds were then air-dried and put in deep freeze chambers at a temperature of -18 to -20 degrees Celsius. At that time, I didn't comprehend the importance of the work being done for the future of the plant kingdom and the benefits which plants bring to all our lives.

This small basic structure was the forerunner of the "Millenium Seed Bank", which is located at Wakehurst Place in Sussex. Part of the RBG Kew, this purpose-built structure aims to provide an insurance policy against the extinction of plants in the wild.

My last job at Kew was to help prune a tall, very wide holly hedge. It must have been about 5 metres across. We had to cut it right back to a leafless skeleton, but to allow time for recovery, it had to be pruned on one side only. The other side would be done next year. George Brown (the Senior Curator who welcomed Pete and I on our first day) came past one day. He stopped, frowned, and with a straight face told us to be very careful. When we asked why, his answer was, 'Black mambas have been seen under there,' and off he went, quietly chortling.

Leaving work on my last day at Kew was a time to reflect on how lucky I had been to spend my practical year's experience at the world's No 1 Botanic Gardens. I had learned new practical skills and acquired invaluable knowledge. In addition, I knew that including time spent at Kew on my *curriculum vitae* would be a job clincher in the future.

After a few weeks spent back home in Soulby, it was back to Writtle for what I thought would be my third and final year of study. As it turned out, that one year would become three.

Nine

Back in Essex for an Extended Stay

Three weeks of summer 1971 were spent back home in Soulby. Enough time to visit family, friends and old familiar places. Then it was back to Writtle for the final year of my diploma course. Ted Heath was the Tory prime minister. On 9th January 1972, the National Union of Mineworkers went on strike for the first time since 1926. Heath declared a state of emergency. The strike lasted for seven weeks. None of the students, me included, seemed the least bit bothered by these events.

Like many other returning students, I decided not to live in college that year. I soon found a place in the nearby village of Sandon. It was a first-floor one-bedroom flat and bathroom with a shared downstairs kitchen. The landlord had an electrical shop in the same building. The ground-floor flat was occupied by a curmudgeonly old boy with Brylcreemed hair and thick-rimmed, dismal brown-coloured National Health-style glasses. He didn't hide his dislike for young people, especially students. The only time he spoke was to grumble about me playing loud music or to make snide comments whenever a girl came to visit.

Conveniently, the King's Head was only 50 metres away. The landlord Paddy Moynihan was an ex-bank manager and chairman of the Licence Victuallers' Association. A portly chap in his early fifties, his most memorable trait was taking snuff whilst serving behind the bar. He would put two small pinches on the top of his right hand, bring his hand up to his nose and then inhale with two sharp intakes through his nostrils. His peroxide blonde wife Pat worked behind the bar with him when she hadn't imbibed too much alcohol. Both were kind to me and before long, I had part-time bar work. Adding up the cost of a large round of drinks tested my mental arithmetic beyond its capabilities. Still, I can't have lost them too much money, because I never got the sack.

Sandon village green was just outside the pub. It was dominated by the canopy of a rare species of oak. Paddy filled me in with some of the tree's history.

'That's a magnificent tree, Paddy.'

He went through his snuff ritual. An act designed to heighten the expectation before he divulged his nuggets of knowledge.

'On the twentieth anniversary of the Queen's Coronation, we parked 144 cars under it.'

'That's incredible. I've never seen a tree as wide as that.'

'The story goes that when it was a sapling, Tommy Wilson, a regular, was staggering home. He lived in that farmworker's cottage.' (Paddy pointed to the other side of the green.) 'He swiped the top clean off with his stick.'

'Well, that would explain why it's the shape it is. What type of oak is it?'

'I was rather hoping you could tell me, David.'

'No idea. I could send a couple of leaves to Kew Gardens and ask them.'

'That's a good idea – they should know.'

I just had to identify the species. Two weeks later, I got my answer. The oak was a specimen of *Quercus castanaefolia*, commonly known as the chestnut-leaved oak.

Trees so special should never be forgotten.

Alistair was Scottish. He was a few years older than me. He worked for the BBC. His job involved servicing aerial installations around the country. Whilst working from his Essex base, he rented a room at the King's Head. We soon became drinking partners. On many occasions, we spread our wings beyond Sandon. Several nights out were spent at the Talk of the South Club in Southend. We saw such legendary acts as the Everly Brothers and Larry Grayson as well as an entertaining hypnotist.

One day stands out as the most memorable but by far the least enjoyable social occasion. We got on a coach full of Alistair's Scottish friends and acquaintances. There must have been thirty. There were cases of beer and bottles of whisky on empty seats, under seats and on the luggage racks. Everyone, except me, had a set of bagpipes. The bus set off and the drinking and musical accompaniment started. The racket never let up until we reached our destination – a pub in the East End of London. Apart from the bar staff, I think I was the only English person in the pub. It was a kind of a bagpipe-themed reunion for exiled Scots. Trying to speak was pointless; the noise was unbearable. On the return journey, the vast quantity of alcohol consumed made the din from the bagpipes ten times worse. The experience coloured my opinion of bagpipes forever.

Ron, a King's Head regular, was a pheasant breeder. Previously, he was involved in the financial sector in Threadneedle Street. During this time, he had accrued considerable wealth. He left the City and was much happier looking after his birds and drinking in the local pub. When paying for drinks, Ron would take out a chunky roll of notes from his back pocket. His nicotine-stained fingers would roll off the required number. He smoked about eighty full-strength Capstan cigarettes a day. No matter how many units of alcohol he'd consumed, he drove off at closing time in his dusty, old brown and cream Morris Traveller.

This year's studies weren't much more demanding than the first year's. I saw this as an opportunity to obtain additional qualifications. It was always my ambition to be awarded the Royal Horticultural Society's National Diploma. There was and still is no higher horticultural accolade. In 1972, I entered the intermediate stage. There were two parts to the examination. Three written papers in which you must gain over 50 percent to proceed to the one-day practical examination. I passed the written and felt extremely confident about the practical element. Most people came unstuck at this stage, but I felt that with thorough preparation, I would succeed. This section was held at the RHS Gardens at Wisley in Surrey. Plant identification was a major component. I visited Wisley three times and learned as many plants as possible. This approach paid off, but the final stage of the diploma would prove far more demanding.

My horticultural knowledge and ability to apply it to new and challenging situations would have to move up a few levels. Fortunately, Writtle ran their Advanced Diploma course which prepared candidates for the RHS National Diploma or Master of Horticulture as it was to become. The course ran every second year with the next one due to start in September 1973. With a year to wait, Writtle employed me as a propagator/nurseryman. Tony Clarke (the Major) was the lecturer in charge. It was a most rewarding twelve months.

***

Tony (as he told me to call him) encouraged and supported me during twelve rewarding months on the Writtle College nursery. My job was propagator/nurseryman. Raising new plants from seeds, cuttings, budding and grafting is the most magical aspect of gardening. Tony was assisted in the day-to-day management by Alan Sparkes, the supervisor. Alan was approaching retirement. Tall with thinning silver hair, he was always very relaxed. His behaviour and personality was in total contrast to Ernie Gasgarth, my first foreman on the nursery at Appleby. In hindsight, Ernie's bullying style instilled in me a strong work ethic and the importance of working to a high professional standard. Alan's gentle ways encouraged me to experiment with methods of propagation and to tackle jobs with thought as opposed to mere repetition.

I raised thousands of plants from cuttings. Most leafy cuttings root readily when they are given warm feet and cool tops. Many of mine were rooted on the mist propagation unit. This system uses a heated bench and overhead sprinklers which deliver a fine mist intermittently. The length and frequency of the spray is determined electronically according to the prevailing weather conditions. More water is sprayed in hot, sunny weather than in cool, cloudy, damp conditions. This keeps the leaves turgid and prevents the rootless cuttings from shrivelling. Once the cuttings have rooted, they are weaned. The mist is gradually stopped.

Shrubs such as hebes and heathers root very easily, whereas others, including rhododendrons and hollies, will only produce roots if the base of the cutting is at a certain stage of ripeness. This stage is reached sometime in August but it varies from year to year. Over the years, a propagator will know when the time is right, by sight and feel. I undertook trials with several species of holly using the technique of wounding, whereby a thin sliver of outer wood is removed on one side from the bottom 25 mm of the cutting. This area was then treated with rooting hormones. I used a range of different strengths and recorded both the speed and strength of the root systems produced. What a privilege it was to be given the time, facilities and encouragement to produce new generations of trees and shrubs.

The young plants were grown on in containers. I was given the freedom to trial different compost mixes and to try various supplementary feeds. The stock looked superb. Tony Clark beamed as he congratulated me. 'Must get the vice principal to come round. It's never looked better,' and off he marched, arms swinging. I felt immensely proud, but thought I could do even better. That was to be my downfall. I gave the plants more feed, and yet more feed.

After a few weeks, and fortunately after Austin Healey the vice principal's visit, the conifers began to go brown. I sheepishly told Alan. When he came to have a look, he asked, 'What have you been feeding them with? How much and how often? I reckon you've overfed them. You're killing them with kindness.'

'Oh hell! What can I do, Alan?'

'Best thing is to get a hosepipe and flood all the containers with gallons of water.'

I repeated this treatment three times. To my relief, it worked, and we only lost a batch of about thirty conifers. I later learned that the excess fertiliser had caused ex-osmosis whereby moisture had come out of the plants to dilute the high concentration of salts in the compost. The plants were drying out.

One hot summer's day, Tony taught me to bud roses. It was a skilful operation. He was very quick and nimble. I was slow and clumsy in comparison, but of course I hadn't his experience. We were joined by Dennis Neate, who had recently joined the teaching staff. Dennis was very reserved and softly spoken. He was taken aback when the watching Tony described the way he was holding the budding knife as being like 'a duchess holding a navvy's tool.'

Dave Feaver was about my age. He also worked in the decorative department under Alan Sparkes. He was the first vegetarian I knew. He and his wife Sandra lived in a cottage in Writtle. Like me, Dave had been accepted onto the Advanced College Diploma course starting in September 1973. Neither of us had the faintest idea how much concentrated study or how many demanding assignments we were to be faced with.

***

The academic year 1973-1974 was and remains the toughest I have experienced. In those days, a full-time course meant exactly that. Lectures and practicals occupied four and a half days a week for thirty-eight weeks. Only Wednesday afternoons were not timetabled. In hindsight, students received full value for money, or we would have done if we had had to pay. Most of us received grants from our local authorities. It really was the best time to be a student.

Demanding assignments were issued to a strict timetable. Late submissions were heavily penalised. Ian Lambert, our course manager, was a dour individual lacking both a sense of humour and the merest hint of leniency. I wasn't his favourite student and always felt that he thought I shouldn't have been selected for the course. I was determined to show old Lambert what I could do by working extremely hard.

Most evenings were spent toiling until 9.30-10 pm. This allowed just enough time to unwind with a couple of pints in the King's Head.

My dedicated approach paid off and I achieved the Advanced Diploma at credit level. Like several of the dozen or so students on the course, I attempted the RHS National Diploma finals. The first section was made up of four three-hour written papers over two consecutive days. To proceed to the practical examination, entrants had to achieve at least 50 percent in each written paper. I didn't succeed, which meant I had to wait another year to try again. Towards the end of this course, it was job-hunting time. After one short listing, I was interviewed and appointed a lecturer in horticulture in Warwickshire. My career was gaining momentum.

Ten

A Time of Life-Changing Events

To be a lecturer had been my long-held ambition. After graduating, I applied for two posts; one in Warwickshire and one in Worcestershire. I felt confident that if I got shortlisted for interview, I would be offered either job. Pershore College of Horticulture invited me to attend for interview. I wasn't chosen. My optimism took a knock. Fortunately, it was a short-lived setback.

Within two weeks, I was heading for my second interview. I drove through impressive gates, past a red brick lodge and down a long, gently winding drive flanked by giant redwoods. An imposing stately home came into view. *What a wonderful place to work, it's amazing* were the first thoughts to enter my head. I parked my mini and climbed the impressive steps leading to the large, solid wooden front door. I was at

Moreton Hall, the home of the Warwickshire College of Agriculture.

I was greeted at the reception by a smiley middle-aged lady. I nervously told her my name and that I had come for interview. She asked if I wanted a coffee and pointed to a seat. It felt like a small, friendly place and just right for starting my teaching career.

Two other candidates joined me. All of us were very guarded, not wishing to give too much away in case we said something that the others could use to their advantage in their interviews.

I was the last candidate to be interviewed. Joyce, the receptionist, ushered me into a large office. Behind a grand, dark wooden desk sat a dapper, little dark-haired man in his mid-thirties. He wore no jacket, no tie and white slacks. His feet were resting on the desk. He got up, shook hands and announced himself.

'My name's George Jackson, the principal and this is Peter Coley the horticultural adviser for Warwickshire. I know where you grew up. Soulby's just a couple of miles from Kirkby Stephen. I spent a few years on a farm at Wharton. Bet you didn't expect that, did you?'

'No, Mr Jackson. I didn't.'

This revelation calmed my nerves slightly. I felt I answered the questions fired at me by both interviewees reasonably satisfactorily.

Following interviews, we were given a tour of the college buildings and grounds. At the far end there was a stable block which had been converted into offices. An equine department, the first at any agricultural college in the country, was thriving. The grounds and greenhouses were like a sleeping giant. Whoever was appointed would be the first horticultural lecturer to be based at Moreton Hall. The Principal wanted that person to revitalise the gardens and create a valuable asset for the college. He pointed out that so long as substantial progress was made, he would not interfere in any way. The original layout of the gardens was largely intact. There was a vast collection of plants. Little maintenance had been carried out over the years, but what a challenge, what potential.

Later that afternoon, I was called back to the office. I was offered the job.

***

My first year in teaching was about 50 percent happy and successful, and the other 50 percent left me wondering if I had chosen the right career.

George Jackson had decreed that the first-year farm students under my tuition would help get the grounds into shape. I had no say in the matter. What George said went. It was the same for every member of staff. He was a dictator – a dictator who not long ago had saved the college from closure. He had total support of the county council to run things as he thought best. He was free to hire and fire staff wherever and whenever he decided. Mr Jackson was a dynamic operator who had moved around the country going from one post to the next more senior post on account of his phenomenal successes.

Teaching agricultural students practical gardening skills was a nightmare. They didn't want to learn anything about gardening. They made that abundantly clear from the outset. They wanted to drive large tractors, milk cows and trim the feet of sheep. I didn't want to be anywhere near them with their ignorant and uncouth behaviour. I was green and nervous, and they relished winding me up by ignoring my attempts to motivate them. One morning, I grabbed this insolent boy by the shoulders and kicked him up the backside. He was unhurt but threatened to report me to the principal. Had he done so, my teaching career would have been over almost before it had begun. I endured this tortuous experience for twelve months.

On Tuesday afternoons, I travelled to the college of further education at Stratford-upon-Avon. I taught a class of about twenty. They were all employed, mostly apprentices from parks departments, nurseries and landscape companies. All were keen to learn and I thoroughly enjoyed my time helping them to gain their City and Guilds qualifications. Another afternoon per week was spent at the college of further education in Leamington Spa. Secondary school pupils went there to learn basic practical gardening skills. They were of mixed ability and their desire to learn variable.

Most of the rest of the week was devoted to work in the grounds of Moreton Hall. I was helped by John Swaffield, a retired farmworker who hailed from the nearby village of Moreton Morrell. John was hardworking and very supportive of my ideas for improvements. A few senior members of the lecturing staff were less than enthusiastic about the changes I was making. The matter was included on the agenda at a staff meeting. It was felt that I was being too ruthless with some of the old shrubberies. George Jackson immediately came to my defence; 'Don't talk so bloody daft. What he's doing is long overdue. He's got my full support… next item on the agenda.' Not a single voice was raised in protest. So I was free to carry on clearing where necessary and replanting to ensure a better future.

Sam was a German who looked after two old wooden greenhouses in which he grew tomatoes. He had worked at the college for many years. A dour old boy of few words and even fewer smiles, he was for some reason allowed to potter at his own pace. I wasn't encouraged to push him hard, but just to let him plod along. He was reliable and never had a day off sick. He lived in a room in the hall and ate in the dining room. I never knew the reasons for his terms of service. I should have been more inquisitive, but back then I didn't want to rock the boat.

The college offered an advisory service for the county's ratepayers. Anyone with a gardening problem could contact us and where possible we gave advice over the telephone. Very often, it was necessary to visit the homeowner's garden to assess the problem. I can vividly recall two visits. The first involved a large wooden greenhouse full of tomatoes which had taken on the most bizarre shapes; some were square, others rectangular with hard green lumps, and none were nice and round. The lady owner looked completely befuddled. 'Bet you've never seen anything like this, young man, have you?'

'Well, no, I haven't, but I think I know what's causing it.' My Writtle training had kicked in; Ian Lambert's lectures on glasshouse crops were about to give me lots of bonus points. 'What have you put in the soil?' I asked.

'Good old horse manure and a bit of bagged fertiliser as usual,' came the reply.

'Does the farmer who supplied the horse manure grow cereals?'

'Well, yes, he does. Why?'

' Bingo! I knew it! He sprays his crops with weed killer, doesn't he?'

'All farmers do, don't they?' she muttered.

I then explained how sensitive tomatoes were to the hormones in weed killers and this was why her tomatoes had gone haywire. On the bright side, if she replaced the soil or grew subsequent crops in isolation from the contaminated soil, she could look forward to healthy tomatoes in future. The worried frown lifted from her face and out came the tea and cakes.

On one occasion, I went to see this Indian man in Leamington Spa. His garden was three-quarters full of garlic; very sickly-looking garlic. I had no idea what was wrong, so I took some samples away and promised to get to the bottom of this disaster. With the help of a colleague, we identified onion white rot as the cause. That was the easy part. I had to tell Mr Patel that there was no cure. 'But you're the expert, you must have a cure. It's our favourite crop, we eat so much garlic.' I resisted the temptation to say *yes, I can smell that*, or to suggest that they move house. It was necessary to explain that the fungus responsible lived in the soil for twenty or more years, and there were no chemicals available to eradicate it. Despite this devastating news, he did make me a cup of tea. Garden visits usually involved tea and biscuits. I often thought that I was like a vicar visiting his parishioners. It was as close as I got to fulfilling my mother's wish for me to enter the clergy.

George Jackson left less than twelve months after I arrived at Moreton Hall. With his career soaring, he was appointed Managing Director of the Royal Agricultural Society. His replacement, Graham Suggett, was a tall, greying, curly-haired Yorkshireman. He had climbed the educational ladder. Principal would be his final destination. He was a fair boss who applied sound reasoning to all his decisions. Under him, the college built firmly on the foundations left by his predecessor.

Around the same time, Peter Coley left. With his Scandinavian wife, Inga, he emigrated to Norway, where he embarked on a new and very different career in the medical profession. Mr Suggett took the opportunity to reorganise horticultural education in the county. The post of County Horticultural Adviser was to be scrapped and replaced by a Head of Horticulture based at Moreton Hall. I could and should have applied for this new post. Lack of confidence and lack of experience meant I thought I wasn't ready for such a senior position. After having a free hand, I then had to answer and obey the successful candidate. I found this new working relationship difficult.

Fortunately for me, the new principal thought it inappropriate for me to try to teach the young farm students practical gardening skills. He did, however, persuade me (different approach to George who always told) to lecture the advanced certificate students about trees, shelterbelts and windbreaks. This required research on my part. However, my lectures were well received; the students could see the benefits of putting the theory into practice on farms.

Through teaching, I had to learn more about many aspects of horticulture. This was extremely beneficial as I was preparing for my second attempt at the Royal Horticultural Societies National Diploma (Master of Horticulture). This time, I was successful.

Over two summer terms in 1976 and 1977, I attended Wolverhampton Technical Teachers' College where I gained my Certificate in Education. It hardly seems believable now but I was seconded on full pay. In my first three years at the Warwickshire College of Agriculture, I had achieved my Master of Horticulture qualification and teaching certificate. I had much to be grateful to the college and both principals for.

***

Decisions made from August 1976 to December 1978 changed the course of my life more drastically than I realised at the time.

During the first two years in Warwickshire, I rented a one-bedroom flat in Leamington Spa. It was relatively cheap but in need of redecorating. Cooking took place in the living room and a bathroom was shared with another tenant. I paid the rent on time and the landlord

(Vince and his wife Mary), who lived on the ground floor, never troubled me, with one notable exception. One night on my return from the pub, their sausage dog came down the hallway yapping and showing its teeth as it flew towards my ankle. I swore and aimed a kick at its backside. The dog yelped and scuttled away. Vince heard the commotion and next day relayed his displeasure at my treatment of their little darling. Despite my insincere apology, the landlord and tenant relationship was strained ever after.

Shortly after the incident with the dog, I was asked if I wanted to be a college warden. This involved living in college rent free in return for extra duties (including supervising students and ensuring they comply with the college rules). Thinking it was an all-gain situation (free food and free accommodation), I accepted.

In August, I moved into my one-bedroom flat in Morton Hall. I shared a massive marble bathroom and a living room with four other members of staff.

***

About this time, my mother was diagnosed with breast cancer. Mam blamed Dad for this. According to her, he whacked her with his elbow, albeit accidently, whilst they were asleep. Whatever the cause, the cancer soon took hold, spreading rapidly.

I visited at the end of every term. The last time I saw Mam was Christmas 1977. She often cried out with pain – it was very distressing. What a horrible way to end your life. I returned to Warwickshire on the 2nd of January 1978. Mam died the following day.

To describe my feelings is difficult. They were so mixed. Yes, I was sad to lose my mother. But she had endured enough pain. Perhaps my strongest emotion was one of relief. A feeling I thought at the time that I shouldn't have. To this day, I still don't think I should have reacted as I did. I felt a sense of freedom. At last I could be myself. My mother's control had been snapped. She always wanted what she considered was the best for me. I felt trapped by her mind-manipulation. The weight of her expectations hung over me like a black cloud. She revelled in boasting about my achievements to friends, neighbours and relatives.

I didn't want to disappoint her, so my life in Warwickshire was in many respects in contrast to that of the son she knew. In Mam's world, drinking alcohol was a terrible sin. She knew I drank when I visited home. Her condemnation went along the lines of 'I know you've been in a pub – I can smell drink on your breath. No good will come of it. It never does.' But she had no idea of the quantity and frequency of my intake whilst away.

She was set against me having girlfriends, claiming it would have a detrimental effect on my career. 'There's plenty of time to find the right girl, someone sensible who will make you a good wife. Look at Joe next door. He was forty when he met Mary.'

'But he's ancient, and she's no oil painting, is she?'

'Yes, well, there are more important things than looks.'

So I took the line that what she didn't know wouldn't harm her. That said, there had only been a few liaisons with the opposite sex, and no serious developments had ensued before she died. Looking back, I can't believe how at the age of thirty I was so weak-willed. I was an introvert trapped in a shell.

I remember nothing about my mother's funeral. Nothing about the journey from Warwickshire to Soulby and back. Nothing about the funeral service. Nothing about the burial in Soulby Cemetery. Nothing about the refreshments afterwards.

**

What happened two days later back in Warwickshire, I recall with great clarity. After lunch, I went to the village pub in Moreton Morrell. I soon got talking to a girl I recognised from college. I knew she was studying horse business management, having seen her around the stable block. That was all I knew about her. She was short, blonde and attractive. It was the start of a long friendship.

Ingrid was five years younger than me. She came from Middlesbrough. She was very calm, controlled, confident and easy to talk to. We stayed friends for many weeks. Then one night our friendship went up a level. After visiting a restaurant in Warwick, we went back to her flat in Moreton Morrell. Whilst in the throes of our first physical encounter, Ingrid discovered the true extent of my baldness. She was understandably shocked, but the discovery didn't cause any lasting damage to our relationship.

In my role as a college warden, I wasn't expected to be involved with a student. Not even a mature student who didn't live in a college hostel and who I didn't teach. I would have lost my job if our association had been exposed.

I had to police the behaviour of residential students. Back then, there were male and female hostels. The two sexes were only allowed to meet in the common rooms. The curfew time was 10.30 pm, when the boys had to return to their own hostels. Gerry Attwood, the senior warden, took great satisfaction in strictly enforcing this rule.

One night, when Ingrid was staying in my room, we heard doors slamming downstairs followed by the unmistakable clop, clop, clop of Gerry's boots as he climbed the stairs. We held our breath and lay motionless. Three loud knocks on the door were followed by 'David, are you in there? There's been some trouble. I need your help.' After what seemed like ages, we heard his retreating footsteps. Nervous laughter broke out.

Next day, Gerry told me, 'We had trouble with some boys from the village last night, David. Did you hear anything? I knocked on your door about twelve thirty!'

'No, nothing, Gerry. I must have been fast asleep,' I replied with trembling voice.

After this close shave, Ingrid and I decided to rent a flat in Leamington Spa. When I wasn't on warden duty, I lived there with her.

In the summer of 1978, we decided it would be exciting to live overseas for a few years. Africa was our chosen destination. I would have to get a job. But I had never seen any horticultural jobs advertised in Africa. Amazingly, within weeks, I found two posts in the magazine *Horticulture Week;* one in Malawi and one in Lesotho. I applied for both. The first to respond was the Overseas Development Agency who invited me to London for interview regarding the post of Senior Lecturer in Horticulture at the Lesotho Agricultural College. To my complete surprise, they offered me the job. My appointment was for two years from January 1979.

This development instigated another major change in our circumstances. For financial (tax) reasons, it was beneficial to marry before we left for Lesotho. We were very happy together, but we weren't in love with each other. We had to become husband and wife in a matter of weeks. A special licence was obtained and the ceremony took place in Northallerton Registry Office in November 1978.

***

The momentous decision of when, where and how was taken for me in a bedroom of the four star Tara Hotel, London. It was early January 1979. The outside temperature was sub-zero. A 4-inch deep layer of solid snow and ice covered the runways. Flights hadn't been able to take off for four days.

I was sitting on the bed waiting for the weather forecast on television. At last, the news that tens of thousands of frustrated passengers had been longing for. 'The big freeze will end tomorrow,' said the newsreader. 'Flights from

Heathrow are expected to get back to normal within two days.'

Ingrid, my wife of two months, got up, grabbed a pair of scissors from her handbag and strode towards me, with that look she had of unmoveable intent. I was as frozen as the ice and snow. So rigid of mind and body that I couldn't escape or protest in any way. She stood in front of me with opened scissors in her right hand and lifted up my lacquered comb over with her left hand. 'Right,' she announced, 'this is it, it's going now.' Within two minutes, my pale, bald pate was exposed. 'Now is the ideal opportunity to accept reality,' she said in a calm, measured tone. 'No one will know you in Lesotho, so there will be no unkind comments and no reason for you to get upset,'

Eventually, I accepted the wisdom of her actions, and my emotions went from trauma to relief. After all, I would have two years at least before anyone in England would see my new hairstyle. We were about to embark on our biggest adventure to date – a new life, a new job, and Africa beckoned.

Eleven

Living the Expatriate Life

I looked across the room and saw sixty African faces. It was the first time I had stood up in front of a class at the Lesotho Agricultural College. The students were silent. I had never experienced anything like this whilst teaching in England. I felt they were waiting for me to deliver great knowledge and wisdom. Did they see me as some kind of messiah?

Right, I thought, *do the usual thing and tell them your name, where you come from and a little about yourself.* One hundred and twenty Basotho eyes were still beamed in on me. I was sweating and my voice trembling. *So*, I thought, *let's try asking their names*. What a pointless exercise that was. How did I imagine I would ever remember all those unfamiliar names? The fact that I tried was, I felt, appreciated. The students were always very polite, always called me sir and had a genuine desire to learn.

The students were on two-year full-time diploma courses. They were being trained as Extension Workers. They came to college without any experience and little or no knowledge, but when they graduated they would take up posts advising farmers and growers in the rural areas of the country.

My job was to educate them in the production of fruit and vegetables which could be grown successfully in this tiny mountain kingdom. Fortunately, I had been given a few days to prepare my first week's lectures. I was ahead of the class, just! Luckily for me, I was able to make use of publications from the South African Advisory Service. Because it is such a large country with wide-ranging climatic conditions, the guidelines given varied from region to region. Those bulletins written for farmers in the Orange Free State were applicable to Lesotho.

Practical classes were the most enjoyable and beneficial part of the training, both for the students and me. Each student was allocated a 2 m by 20 m plot on which to grow vegetables. This area, complete with a water supply, was adjacent to the college entrance road. I worried myself silly thinking that if these plots weren't bursting with bountiful vegetables it would reflect my ability to inspire. My success or failure would be there for public scrutiny. I had arrived in winter. This meant there was enough time to set out the ground and prepare for seed sowing.

The basic principles of crop husbandry varied little from those followed at home. It was a case of adapting to a new climate and getting familiar with different varieties. Crops included beans, carrots, beetroot, turnips, potatoes and Swiss chard. Peppers, tomatoes and squash needed protection in their early stages when grown at home. In Lesotho, they were sown directly into the soil, where they grew rapidly to maturity. Pests and diseases were almost non-existent. There was no need for insecticides and fungicides. Crops were grown organically long before it became popular in Britain.

By the end of my contract, I had long since realised that there were two fundamental principles that needed to be got across to the students. Firstly to keep weeds under control and, even more importantly, to add as much organic matter as possible to the soil. This could come from animal manure. However, as dung was dried for fuel, the making of compost stood the greater chance of success.

The college farm land was located next to the buildings and adjacent to the Caledon River. Part of the land was irrigated from the river and some crops were grown dry without any extra water. A large area was devoted to maize. This was the major crop of Lesotho. It formed the basis of *mealie* meal; the staple food of the Basotho. The college farm also grew *lucerne* (a legume used for animal fodder) and *sorghum,* which was used to make beer. The beer was often sold in *shebeens* (illegal drinking dens which the authorities failed to police). The effects of this beer were often disastrous. Heavy drinkers could be recognised by their blurred, cloudy eyes – blindness usually ensued.

The small orchard was situated on a raised piece of ground above the river. My predecessor had chosen the ideal site. It faced the sun and wasn't liable to frost damage at blossom time. Practical classes were limited to twelve students. It was a chance to get to know the individuals. I picked up a few words and phrases of Sesotho. In hindsight, I wish I had tried harder to speak their language and to understand their way of life more fully.

One day, when in the orchard, darkness fell rapidly. Fork lightning soon followed. I was scared. The students looked petrified. They were talking rapidly in Sesotho. I asked them why they were so agitated.

'I thought you would be used to violent electric storms! You get lots of them in the mountains, don't you?'

'The witch doctors are angry. They are joining the sky to the earth, sir,' said a student.

I guess he could sense the fear I was feeling when I unconvincingly retorted, 'You don't believe in witch doctors, do you?'

'Oh yes, sir. Anyone who doesn't will be punished.'

We made a hasty retreat back to the classroom.

The campus was being developed along the lines of Bishop Burton College in East Yorkshire. Keith Younger, the principal, used the design of the library, domestic science building and the machinery workshops as templates. Keith took great pride in the appearance of the grounds. He asked me to take control and introduce more plants. He wanted more roses. Another little bit of England was emerging in the southern hemisphere.

The college management paralleled the English system with a principal, vice principal, senior lecturers and lecturers. Expatriates held all the senior posts. The intention was for the local staff to take over the running of the college at the end of our contracts.

Staff meetings and section meetings were regularly held. Every fourteen days, I attended the farm meeting. Developments were discussed and progress analysed. One aspect has stuck in my memory. Every member of staff with responsibility for livestock had to give a headcount.

Mr Motsoene the vice principal chaired the meeting. He went around the table asking for numbers.

'How many sheep do we have, Mr Lekatsa?'

'About eighteen,' came the reply. It was never an exact number.

Peter Roberts always remarked that 'it either was or wasn't eighteen.'

At which point, Lekatsa became fidgety and evasive, coming out with comments like, 'They were moving around a lot so it was difficult to say for sure.'

Peter knew as everyone else did that Lekatsa wouldn't divulge the exact number because he siphoned a few off to take home from time to time.

***

Days were always hot and dry in winter. The countryside was brown and bare. Lesotho was and still is one of the least forested countries in Africa with only 1 percent of the land covered in trees. On an August day in 1979, we embarked on a journey to the top of this land-locked mountain kingdom.

The local guidebook advised against taking this trip unless your vehicle was in tip-top condition. As instructed, I checked the petrol, water, oil and tyre pressures of our beige Vauxhall Cavalier which the Overseas Development Administration had imported for us. It would take at least five hours to reach our destination.

We passed the tiny airport with its five seven-seater planes which serviced a few airstrips in the remote parts of the country. Then we proceeded on tarred roads through the capital Maseru, which stands at 1,600 metres above sea level. Before long, the road turned into a rutted track with deep potholes and numerous large, sharp stones to negotiate, without a sump guard or a cattle bar. We started to climb to over 3000 metres. The spectacular Drakensburg and Maluti mountains on the northern border of Lesotho and South Africa beckoned.

The road twisted and turned up the Blue Mountain Pass. I looked over the side of the unfenced track. The deep ravine was littered with the remains of lorries and *bakkies* (pick-up trucks). Some were teetering on rocky ledges before they tumbled to the bottom. How many dead or seriously injured drivers, I mused?

'Bloody hell, look at all those!'

'You keep your eyes on the road. Stay away from the edge,' said a calm-sounding Ingrid.

Near the top, the road forked. Without a signpost, we had no idea which way to go. On the horizon there were three *rondavels*. These small, round thatched buildings made up a family home. We drove towards them. An old man wrapped in the customary Basotho blanket and riding a sure-footed Basotho pony approached the car. A smile broke out across his deeply furrowed, leathery face as he greeted us in Sesotho. '*Lumela, me, khotso, ntate.*' ('Good day, madam, and good day, sir,' in English.) The Basotho people living in the country were far friendlier than the town dwellers. They always asked how you were?– '*U kae*' – and wanted to know where you had come from and were going to. He pointed in the direction of Thaba-Tseka and said goodbye, wishing us well ('*Sala hantle*').

A few kilometres further on, we entered a long valley. A roaring wind brought thick clouds of dust swirling towards the car. This was being blown off freshly ploughed fields. August is very windy and dry. It is known as the dust month. We immediately closed all windows and ventilators, but soon a layer of pulverised brown earth covered ourselves and the car's interior.

Soil erosion in Lesotho is catastrophic. As well as wind, there is water erosion. The spring months of September and October are very wet. We would not have been able to make this journey then. Torrential downpours accompanied by violent thunderstorms cause flash flooding. Deep rills quickly appear on the soil surface. With no vegetation to bind the soil, the rills soon become massive chasms known as "*dongas*". Soil is washed away and ends up in the rivers. The reasons for this irreversible loss of soil are many and varied. Aid agencies have tried planting trees to stabilise the land. Sadly, yet understandably, the Basotho people cut down the trees for fuel to cook with and to provide heat. Cow dung, which would provide valuable organic matter for the soil, is dried and burned. Anyone with livestock was allowed to graze the community-owned land. This resulted in most areas being overgrazed. The scarred, weather-worn landscape was considered by many Basotho to be normal; they thought it was like that in every country.

Next stop was Thaba-Tseka, the capital and only town in the district of the same name. After refreshments, we headed north along a wide valley. Soon the sides became closer and we climbed higher towards the towering Drakensburg Mountains, which border Natal. The temperatures plummeted; car windows were tightly closed and heating set to maximum. We didn't want to travel in darkness which descended suddenly at about 7 pm every day of the year. With two hours to spare, we reached "Oxbow Lodge" and checked in for the night. The accommodation was, as expected, basic but clean. It was bitterly cold outside and not much warmer inside. We hadn't brought sufficient warm clothes. With snow covering the mountaintops, it looked every bit the idyllic ski resort which the government claimed it to be. Back then, it had one T-bar lift and was only reachable in a 4-wheel drive vehicle.

Next day, following a shivering night's lack of sleep, we returned home. As always, the journey home never seemed to take as long as getting there. I was mightily relieved to complete this adventure safely, without accident or breakdown. That night, I told Ingrid about my temporary car repair. Whilst adjusting the car's timing, I had cracked the rotor (an integral little part which was responsible for igniting the fuel). This tiny but crucial part spun round rapidly. It could have broken in two any time on the journey. Being a British car, a spare rotor wasn't available in Southern Africa. My solution was to bind it together with Sellotape. Upon hearing this disclosure, she let rip. 'You didn't think to tell me. We could have been stranded up there. At the mercy of the weather. Maybe robbed by locals, or worse.'

'Oh well, we got back safely,' was my feeble response.

***

The sun powered down on the roof of our car, just like it did for 300 days of the year. We drove along a straight, dusty track. Soon we came to a sandstone, tin-roofed bungalow. Nothing had disturbed the sparse vegetation of kikuyu grass and scrub leading to the front porch (or *stoep* in Afrikaans) for years. Brown, crisped-up camellia leaves were piled up to the front door, and a thin film of orange soil had settled on the windows.

We'd been told the key would be under an old stone pot. Sure enough, it was. It was a heavy, rusty piece of iron, but it worked. Once inside the dingy house, we saw that the ivy had grown through the walls and its roots poked their way through the wallpaper. There was a good-sized kitchen with an Aga-type stove, a living room and three bedrooms. We could tart the place up and deal with the ivy.

A walk around the 6-acre garden clinched the deal. There was a small orchard with about a dozen peach and nectarine trees. Prickly pears were growing around a plot which looked like a one-time vegetable garden. But the real decider was a lean-to building which Ingrid could use as a stable. At 50 rand a month (£30) and only thirty minutes' drive from Maseru, it would be the ideal weekend retreat. Ingrid could get a horse and go riding with her friend Claire. It was Claire who suggested this place. Claire and Bernard Amm (she was French and he was Lebanese) were farmers near the small town of Ladybrand in the Orange Free State. Their farm was a ten-minute drive away.

Facilities at our second home were basic. Nothing as easy as flicking a switch or turning on a tap. The water supply came from a borehole. Water had to be pumped to a raised tank near the house. This meant starting an old Lister diesel engine, which was often temperamental. The water was gravity fed into the house so the pressure wasn't great. Electricity was supplied by four large black batteries housed in a shed near the back door. Another diesel engine charged the batteries. They only generated enough electricity to run the lights. When the batteries were getting low, the lights would quickly fade. That was my cue to start the infernal combustion engine.

Our refrigerator was fuelled by paraffin. It was tricky to light and had to be positioned so that a draught didn't blow out the flame.

The telephone was like the type seen on *Dr. Finlay's Casebook*. We were on a joint line with several farms. To dial a number, you turned a handle next to the receiver. Each number had its own ring pattern. For a long ring, you turned the handle three times and for a short ring, only once. Our number had three longs and two shorts.

There was a large, round concrete reservoir near the house which doubled up as a swimming pool. It was most likely a remnant from the days when the bungalow was part of a large farm. A crack in the bottom meant it regularly needed topping up from the borehole. I didn't use it much, but Ingrid loved floating in it when she was pregnant with our first child.

We employed two garden boys, not because we needed them, but because it was expected of the rich white people to provide employment for the blacks. They were both very happy, hardworking boys. Most importantly, they were excellent snake catchers. Snakes were a highly desirable source of food. They were welcome to it. We were never tempted.

We grew our own meat in the form of a pig. Pig meal was supplemented with peaches, which it adored. The pig was housed in a rickety shed from which it frequently escaped. It would come to the back door and make loud, squeaky noises until it was given peaches. The end result from this fruity diet was a freezer full of very sweet meat.

Prickly pears proved to be a very valuable form of currency. I thought they tasted like a bar of soap. The Basotho thought they were delicious. Boxes full of these egg-shaped, pale green/yellow prickly fruits loaded in the car boot eased our passage through the border post. Whites going from Lesotho to the Republic were waved through by the Afrikaans border guards with the minimum delay. Blacks and their vehicles were thoroughly checked and made to wait unnecessarily. When whites entered Lesotho, the Basotho guards got their revenge. Whites were thoroughly checked and made to wait for ages. On one occasion, they asked me to open the boot. When they saw the contents, they became animated; their faces lit up. The Head Honcho looked at me and with optimism in his voice exclaimed, 'You have many nice prickly pears, sir – so many! Who will eat all those?'

'Would you like some, *ntate*?'

'You are very kind person, sir.'

I handed him a small boxful and he waved me through. The rest I sold to the Spa supermarket in Maseru. I had come across swift entry through the border post. Our two-home lifestyle was blissful. After two months this euphoric existence would suffer a severe jolt.

***

Weekends were spent over the border. All went well for twelve weeks until we arrived back in Maseru one Monday morning. As we got near the front door of the bungalow, we noticed that all the curtains were closed. We hadn't left them like that. I opened the front door and switched the lights on. Dozens of spent matches littered the floor. Our eyes circled the living room. We looked at each other in disbelief. We had been burgled. Every room had been cleaned out. Ingrid was pregnant with our first child. All the baby's things and pram bought in readiness for the arrival had gone. Even the dog's bed had been taken. It was the most distressing experience; a feeling of total violation. Our only possessions were in the farm bungalow.

The neighbours rallied round with the usual words like *it could have been worse* and *come and have a cup of tea*. Later that morning, I got myself sufficiently together to report the burglary to the police. I drove to the police station. Officialdom in Lesotho moved like a geriatric snail. After a long delay, the sergeant produced a form and began asking me questions like, 'Which tribe do you belong to?'

To which I somewhat stroppily replied, 'I'm British!' Then he asked if I could drive them to the scene of the crime. They didn't have a spare vehicle. Four of them piled in. We stopped at the traffic lights (Maseru's only set). One of the officers called out to two men in the street. They also jumped in the car. I was told they were the fingerprint experts.

At the bungalow, they wandered around muttering in Sesotho. They appeared clueless. I pointed out a broken window where the thieves had gained entry and suggested they check for fingerprints. It later transpired that theft from expatriates was considered fair game and was part of organised crime, which went to the heart of government. The police were under orders not to delve too deeply into house burglaries. Stolen goods were taken by truck into the Orange Free State. We never saw any of our possessions again.

We had no choice but to live full time over the border in the cottage. Due to its isolated location, we needed a second car. I bought a very cheap, barely roadworthy VW Beetle for travelling between work and home.

***

Our health care was funded by the National Health Service. Whenever we needed it, we received first-class treatment in South Africa. We were recommended by the British High Commission and other expatriates to use the surgery and cottage hospital in Ladybrand.

Dr Lamprecht and Dr Strauss were both in their thirties. Lamprecht was the taller of the two. He sported a moustache and spoke with a broader AfriKaan's accent than the dark-haired, bearded Dr Strauss. The smell of cigarettes pervaded their surgery. Weak swirls of dwindling smoke were sometimes seen as you entered. Their extinguished smokes had been hastily put into an ashtray and shoved in the desk drawer. They were, however, excellent doctors.

My first visit was the result of a seized-up back. I had bent down to get a mug out of a bottom cupboard and couldn't straighten up. My lower back had locked. Somehow I managed to get into the car. Ingrid drove me to the surgery. Dr Lamprecht told me to loosen my shorts and lie face down on the couch. He pulled my shorts down and inserted a needle into my lower back.

'Just lie there for one minute and you will be able to get up and move freely,' he said. 'Okay, up you get!'

True enough, I got up with no trouble; it was a miracle treatment. God knows what was in that needle but it worked, and quickly. He gave me a tube of ointment to apply if I had any more back problems. It had an unforgettable name – Thrombo Flob Gell.

Sunday, 24th Feb 1980 saw the birth of our first daughter, Rachel. Ingrid was about two weeks overdue, but the doctors were relaxed about it.

'It will arrive when it's good and ready,' Dr Strauss had proclaimed.

At about seven o'clock, just as darkness fell, Ingrid called from the bedroom, 'You better take me to hospital straight away.'

'Why, what's matter? What's the hurry?'

'This baby won't wait much longer, that's why!'

Within half an hour, we were in Ladybrand Cottage Hospital. My wife was taken to a delivery room and they called Dr Strauss. He had been playing golf and was relaxing in the clubhouse. He duly arrived, still dressed in his sporty clothes, said hello to me and went through to Ingrid.

There was no way I wanted to be there at the birth. I knew I would be useless and probably faint. I waited outside, pacing up and down the corridor; all the time smoking constantly. Why was it taking so long?

At 11 pm, a nurse came out and said, 'You have a daughter. She weighs seven and a half pounds; both mother and baby are in good health. You can go and see them.'

When I first saw our baby, my reaction was one of shock.

I said nothing until later, when I had left the room. I asked a nurse, 'Why has she got a pointed head?'

'Oh, that's perfectly normal immediately after birth. It will soon get more rounded, you will see.'

To my great relief, she was right, and a few days later I brought mother and daughter home.

***

Nearly a year after the burglary, we moved back to Maseru and into another college bungalow. This one was next door to our previous home. The novelty of battling with diesel pumps to recharge batteries and fill up water tanks had waned.

All seven properties were identical. It was a real pleasure to have the convenience of mains electricity and mains water again. It was a five-minute walk to work. Our neighbours included four English families, one American couple and one with an American wife and a German husband.

We spent most evenings outside socialising with the neighbours. Large quantities of cheap but excellent beer and wine were consumed. Often, this helped to wash down food cooked on a *braai* (Afrikaans for barbeque). Cooking appliances were basically made out of bisected oil drums, heated with wood and fitted with grills on which food was cooked. The large expatriate population in Maseru bought into *braais* in a big way.

Each bungalow was set in a half-acre plot. I turned part of ours into a vegetable garden. Crops grew so easily and quickly. I dug the ground, sowed seeds, watered regularly, and in a very short time we had tasty tomatoes, piquant peppers, shiny aubergines, succulent sweetcorn (delicious when wrapped in foil and roasted

Rachel in Lesotho 1980

on the braai), crunchy carrots, massive watermelons and wonderful butternut squashes.

Electrical storms were commonplace. Spectacular displays of sheet and fork lightning filled the vast sky. On one occasion, when a storm was directly overhead, a booming roar of thunder saw the dinner plates dance and rattle on the table. Later that same evening as we lay in bed, violent fork lightning blew the plugs of the bedside table lamps out of their sockets. Scorch marks around the pinholes reminded us of this close encounter.

We experienced another impressive light display one night just before sunset. Sitting in the Kings' front garden, drinking as usual, we saw large arc lights the other side of the Caledon River. They must have been 100 ft tall and for several minutes they kept criss-crossing.

'It's over the border in the Republic,' reckoned Alan King.

'What do you think it is, Alan?' asked Peter Roberts.

'Haven't a clue, Peter.'

'Well, I think it's a UFO, it's a bloody UFO!' I chirped up.

'No! – you don't believe in that nonsense,' chortled Peter.

'Have you got a better explanation?'

A few days later, Peter claimed to have heard on good authority that my UFO was the South African Defence Force carrying out manoeuvres. I chose not to believe this disappointing explanation.

Just before my two-year contract was up, I was offered a six-month extension. The young Basotho lecturer who was destined to replace me was studying horticulture at Pershore College in Worcestershire. He still had six months to complete his course. I was offered yet another pay increase if I agreed to stay until July 1981. My salary went up almost 30 percent in two years. I accepted gleefully.

Basotho staff were being trained to fill the senior posts held until now by expatriates. Peter Roberts, the Senior Lecturer in Agriculture, and his wife and children went back to Shropshire in January 1981. The bungalow they had occupied remained empty for several months. Thefts of furniture and fittings still happened at frequent intervals. Keith Younger, the principal, was sure that the Roberts' old house would soon be targeted. Keith was a small, skinny man who always shunned confrontation. He had been chosen by the ODA as a safe pair of hands to lead the college smoothly towards total Lesotho management. Against his normal mode of operation, he persuaded me to join him one night to sit in wait of the robbers.

Armed with hockey sticks (supplied by Keith's wife Jean), we crouched behind the settee and waited for the robbers to break in. We were both shaking with fear.

'What do we do if anyone comes, Keith? What if they are armed?'

'They will be so shocked when we jump up brandishing our weapons, they will flee.'

To our great relief, no one showed. Keith never suggested we repeat this stupid exercise.

We had to leave the bungalow two days before we were due to fly back to the UK. Accommodation was provided for us in a Maseru hotel. It was one of those occasions when you always remember where you were when a major event took place. This time it was 29th July 1981 and the wedding of Prince Charles to Lady Diana was being shown on the hotel television. Time was dragging and there was nothing better to do than watch most of it.

I also had time to reflect on how useful or otherwise my contribution and the impact of overseas aid had been to Lesotho and its people. My deliberations were then incorporated into the end-of-contract report which I was required to complete for my employer, namely the Overseas Development Agency. The gist of what I tried to convey was as follows.

***

During my time in Lesotho, millions of pounds of foreign aid poured into this poverty-stricken country. The agricultural college where I worked was transformed with new buildings. It looked as though it had been lifted by a giant crane in England, then lowered into the dusty earth, clear blue skies and searing sun of Southern Africa. Machinery workshops were kitted out with the latest farm equipment and large tractors. All of which was impressive on the eye, but of little if any benefit to most of the rural population. Basotho farmers were given tractors. Having little money to purchase fuel resulted in these expensive machines standing idle for most of the year. A lack of training for the drivers meant that when the tractors were occasionally used, they often turned over on the steep-sided, mountainous terrain.

Such accidents resulted in many deaths. The sure-footed Basotho ponies were more versatile and didn't have the cost and dangers associated with tractors.

I had taught the production of fruit and vegetables at a level which involved hand tools and hand labour. It was therefore appropriate to the needs of the small-scale farmers of Lesotho. They could afford the tools and seeds required to produce a more varied and healthy range of food for their families. The success of the system would depend on the extension workers who were taught at the college taking their knowledge and skills out into the country. The biggest concern was how long it would be before many of these ex-students would be tempted by the considerably larger wages to be earned working in the mines of South Africa.

In Maseru, foreign aid money was invested in hotels, a cinema and a casino. Every Friday, Afrikaaners would cross the border into Lesotho to indulge passions forbidden to them in apartheid South Africa, namely gambling and pornographic films. The money they spent wasn't much help for the ordinary Basotho people.

In 1981, only about 20 percent of the population had access to electricity and most of these were in three urban areas, including the capital, Maseru. Fortunately, the bungalow which came with my job had mains electricity, water and the telephone.

Four-fifths of the population lived in basic little stone-built houses called *rondavels*. The stones were held together with a mix of soil and cow dung. Roofs were thatched and the flooring made from compressed dung and earth.

Light and heat for cooking came from kerosene lamps. When darkness fell, about 7 pm, families wrapped in their colourful woollen Basotho blankets would huddle together for warmth. Children suffered from eye strain as they tried to read and do their homework by the dull, flickering light produced by burning noxious kerosene. Thick black smoke filled the houses, which caused serious lung damage and eye infections for all the family. The lamps made from old food cans, or even pressurised aerosols, were easily knocked over. Fires were a common disaster and put lives and possessions at risk. Kerosene is poisonous clear liquid often sold in clear bottles. It was easily mistaken for water by children. A high proportion of the family budget was spent on this fuel, thereby squeezing the noose of poverty even tighter.

***

Thirty-nine years on, my reminiscences led me to wonder if living conditions for the majority of Basotho families had improved. From what I can discover, little has changed in the rural areas. Only 6 percent of households are connected to the national grid.

Solar technology has advanced immensely in recent years. In a country like Lesotho, with 300 days of sunshine a year and at least twelve hours of sun a day, the harnessing of solar power should be blindingly obvious. Yes, there is a cost for renewable energy! Lithium has to be mined for batteries and solar panels have to be made. But unlike dirty, polluting oil and coal, these costs aren't continuous.

Having installed solar panels on our roof in Carlisle in 2013, I know how beneficial they are, even in Cumbria. My enthusiasm led me to discover the charity SolarAid. Being a relatively small charity, it doesn't have massive overheads. For every £1 given, 90p is spent for the benefit of local people in Malawi, Uganda and Zambia. I contacted SolarAid's small London office to say I worked in Lesotho around 1980, and to ask, 'When will you be distributing lights to Lesotho?'

'As soon as funds allow, our work will spread to other countries. I will let you know when we are operating in Lesotho.'

SolarAid is distributing affordable solar lamps into rural Africa through their social enterprise SunnyMoney. Costing around £3 each, that's a big saving on the price of kerosene. These small, light, portable lamps give out much brighter, steadier light than kerosene lamps. They provide a clean, safe source of light. They don't create pollution or carbon emissions. Children use them to read and do their homework. Money saved enables families to spend more on seeds and fertilisers. Crop yields and family health improve.

Help is as local as it's possible to get. Help is instant – there is no waiting for an electricity grid system which may never come. Six hundred million people in Africa (that's more than eleven times the population of England) rely on kerosene lamps for light. SolarAid's aim is to consign their use on the African continent to the history books by 2030. If you have never known life without electricity, this may seem easily achievable until you focus on the vast numbers of people who have never flicked a light switch.

Twelve

Return to England

W e left Maseru on the 31st of July 1981. Winter in Lesotho was dry; nights were cold. The landscape was brown and barren, like a mountainous desert. We were met at Teesside Airport by Ingrid's sister, her brother, his wife and two children and her mother. What joy it was to walk off that plane and see, smell and walk in the fresh green land of our birth. After two and a half years, we were home. It felt so good! It looked and felt small! After the vastness of Africa, the towns and villages seemed squashed together, as if squeezed by the hands of a giant. But it was cosy. It was great to be back.

We were driven to her mother's house in the attractive village of Hutton Rudby in North Yorkshire. She lived in an old renovated farmhouse. Her husband – Ingrid's father – had been a master builder. I never met him. He had just finished working on the house when he died from a heart attack, aged fifty. It was to be our home for the next three months.

Finding a job was my number one priority. It wasn't long before I got an interview for a lecturer's post in Wath-upon-Dearne, South Yorkshire. As I approached the area, a dark cloud of despondency descended above my head like an avalanche hurtling down the Alps. The area was dour; buildings were ingrained with decades of coal dust and shopfronts were boarded up. House windows were so dirty that those that were occupied let in very little natural light. Inside must have been almost as dark as down the pits. You could almost smell the feeling of hopelessness in this once-bustling industrial area. I had a powerful urge to turn the car round and get out of this utterly depressing town. It was without enthusiasm that I attended for interview at the Rockingham College of Further Education. I was offered and accepted the job.

Under a government scheme, the college was paid handsomely to provide courses and thereby artificially lower the unemployment rate. Facilities for teaching horticulture were virtually non-existent. With a few hand tools and some areas of uninspiring municipal-style shrub planting, I was timetabled to teach a group of twelve, mostly male sixteen-to eighteen-year-olds, the rudiments of horticulture every morning. They were very disgruntled with their lot in life. Coal mines in the area were, one by one, having their life support switched off. When they left school, the young males wanted to go down the local pit like their fathers and grandfathers had done. They felt it was their inheritance.

They didn't want to leave the town. Where would they find work if they did? Their behaviour resembled that of hefted sheep. Their prospects didn't seem any brighter than those of the young people of Lesotho. At least they could find work in the mines of South Africa. Trying to get those Yorkshire lads interested in gardening was a challenge which I failed to meet. When I managed a modicum of crowd control, it seemed like a successful morning.

Afternoon sessions were in stark contrast. The steelworks in Sheffield had closed. European money poured into the college. Workers had been given a decent redundancy package as part of a retraining programme. The group of nine males, aged from fifty to sixty-five, were a pleasure to spend time with. All were interested in learning more about gardening. Three were already fairly knowledgeable.

We took over an empty allotment site on the edge of town. The pungent, bituminous-like stench of the nearby coking plant was an almost constant accompaniment. Like most examples of the coal industry, it would be consigned to industrial heritage within a few years.

The men loved working outside. After the intense heat of the blast furnaces, it must have been bliss. Soon the site was akin to an RHS model kitchen garden. The good-natured banter and the challenges they set each other regarding work targets were morale boosters. Tommy, the oldest and most respected member of the team, would regularly pronounce, 'Job and done.' The upshot of this meant that when the day's tasks were done, they could all go to the pub and sink a few pints.

Even the afternoons couldn't make up for the fact that working in this college fell far short of the satisfaction I had previously experienced in Warwickshire and Lesotho. But it was a job. I was grateful for that, but I was determined to move to a more fulfilling post in an attractive location before long.

Whenever I think back to those days, I remember the words of the comedian, singer and broadcaster Mike Harding. A colleague of mine related the story of Mike performing his one-man show near Wath. He allegedly announced that 'Wath is twinned with Krakatau. It was the only place that Hitler didn't bomb, because he thought that it looked as if it had already been done.'

Buying a house in the area wasn't a consideration. We rented a bungalow 8 miles from college in Worsbrough Dale, near Barnsley. We lived there for eight months.

Then the cards fell kindly for us. The post of Head of Horticulture at Broomfield College (the Derbyshire College of Agriculture) became vacant. I applied and was called for interview. The college was based in the rural parish of Morley, just outside Derby. As I drove towards Broomfield Hall, I wanted this job. The hall was an attractive old building within several acres of landscaped gardens, including a walled garden. The estate was composed of several hundred acres of farmland. There was great potential to improve the horticultural facilities and vastly increase the number and breadth of courses on offer. This was the challenge I knew I could rise to. I confidently sailed through the interview and was offered the position. I was delighted to accept. After ten months in

Wath-upon-Dearne, it felt like sunshine bursting through after prolonged rain. We were on the move.

***

It was mid-September 1982. The first day in my new post, and the principal – Ernie (Ernest Victor James) Bathurst, sometimes known as eevejebee – introduced me to the members of the horticultural teaching staff for whom I was to be responsible. I felt a strong sense of resentment in the atmosphere. They both thought they should have been offered the job. I would need skin as thick as animal hide. Two days later, I met the other member of staff. She was part time and couldn't have been more welcoming. The balance was redressed somewhat. It felt good to have an ally.

I was given my own office and my own secretary. Those were the days before computers. Wendy was the expert who did the typing and filing. I spent my time doing what I was best qualified to do and what I was appointed for. At thirty-five years of age, my confidence for the challenge knew no bounds. I immediately set to work planning my targets and the means to achieve them. Horticulture at Broomfield College had been limping along for decades. Due to the large urban population in the neighbouring towns from which to recruit, student numbers could multiply manyfold. We needed to introduce more attractive courses and improve the marketing to reach more employers, their workforces and potential students.

This explosion in student numbers would require more teaching staff and improved teaching facilities. My vision of an empire was taking shape. Money to turn it into reality would be a major stumbling block, according to Mr Bathurst. He applauded my ambition but urged caution.

'The Horticultural Development Committee will not advocate investing much money in new facilities. How much do you think it will take to implement your plans?'

'One hundred thousand pounds should do it, Mr Bathurst.'

'What! How much? You may as well whistle, fella! Still, make your case with full costings and see what they agree to. The next meeting is in four weeks' time – Monday, 10th October.'

There were six members of the committee, including two who had been part of my interview panel. Frank Constable, a retired director of Derby Parks, was Chairman. Frank was a diplomat. Rather than confrontation, he took the path of gentle cajoling in his efforts to reach decisions on controversial matters. Charles Binham ran a local garden. His red beard looked like a crow's nest at sunset. With his booming voice, Charles was forceful in his opinions.

'We've been the Cinderella to the farmers for too long. It's high time this college did something for horticulture.'

He was looking forward to a transformation. I reckoned it was wise to keep him on side even if his forthright opinions might not always be well received.

The most influential member was Stan Mellors. Stan was Chairman of the Governors. I had not met him prior to the meeting. He was a retired miner and member of the

County Council's ruling Labour Party. The most important thing from my point of view was that Stan loved plants and immediately offered me his full support.

With the meeting underway, I presented my plans. These included: a new glasshouse block, a large new teaching building exclusively for horticulture, the establishment of a plant nursery together with the associated growing facilities and investment in tools, equipment and machinery. Frank thanked me for my presentation and I sat down.

Then came the crunch! 'How much will all this cost?' asked Frank.

'One hundred thousand pounds,' I blurted out.

The silence seemed to last forever. Eventually, old Frank muttered something along the lines of, 'Where do you think all this money will come from?'

All heads except Stan's and mine were shaking.

Stan looked up, pushed back his slender, forward-facing shoulders and said, 'Let's not be too hasty. You don't get owt for nowt, and that goes for you, young man.'

He looked directly at me as he spoke. 'I suggest we find the money and release it in instalments over the next three years. In return, you will have to repay some of the investment with the money coming from more students and by selling plants grown on the nursery you have proposed. I wouldn't expect a profit, just a partial return for the council's money.'

He then looked across the table and telling rather than asking, delivered the clinching line: 'I'm sure you can find the money somewhere, Frank.'

A flustered Frank replied, 'I will have to consult the Ways and Means Committee.'

I was to discover that this was Frank's stock answer whenever he was charged with finding money. I never did find out whether this committee actually existed.

That didn't matter, for I had been given the green light. Could I live up to the expectations bestowed upon me, or had I set myself unachievable goals?

After the meeting, Stan asked me if I could get him seeds of a plant he had recently seen growing in Cornwall.

'It's called Chilean bellflower, *Lapa* something or other. I wrote the name down. Hang on, I've got it in my wallet. Here it is – *Lapageria rosea*. It's a cracker! Do you know it?'

'Oh yes! I remember it in the Temperate House at Kew,' I replied, without conviction.

'So it should be fine in my conservatory. See if you can get me some seeds then.'

This was my first challenge and fortunately I tracked down a source of the seeds within a week. I proudly handed them to Stan at the next meeting.

***

We bought our first house on the outskirts of Derby in 1982. It was a three-bedroom detached bungalow. Two miles from work on a quiet road. We had a good-sized front garden and a large rear garden – about a quarter of an acre in total. The almost new red cedar greenhouse was, for me, the star attraction.

Unfortunately, the bungalow failed to live up to our expectations. The previous owner had been a DIY fanatic but, sadly for us, a very poor example. The central heating system installed by said owner and his son constantly needed adjusting and bleeding. This was due to the wrong bore water pipes being used.

I learnt from Bert next door that Mr Odd Job made decorative walling blocks – the sort that were popular in the '60s and '70s.

'George was always trying his hand at something. Messing about with old cars. As for all those concrete blocks he made – trouble was, he made them very badly. Never got the mix right. Most of them crumbled.'

'So what happened to them?'

'Don't know – David… they had a massive tidy-up before the bungalow went on the market, so must have got rid of them, then.'

When I decided to turn some of the back garden into a vegetable plot, I found hundreds of broken ones buried just below the surface. Ernie Bathurst let me borrow a tractor and trailer at the weekends to cart them away. In return, I was to tip the blocks into a couple of muddy, badly drained college farm gateways. Three days and six trailer loads later, the vegetable plot was ready for final preparations.

Our biggest problem was damp – rising damp. Water used to run down the bedroom walls. Wallpaper bubbled and came away from the walls. This exposed the recently renewed electric wiring. Rather than being set into the walls, it stood proud, and the raised track could be seen where plaster had been applied to cover the cables.

Eighteen months after moving in, our second daughter Laura was born. It was 21st February 1983. In the spring of 1984, we decided that the damp problem was too expensive to fix. We applied a coat of paint and new wallpaper and hoped for a quick sale.

I put a handmade *For Sale* board up in the front garden. Within days, there was a knock at the front door. A couple in their fifties from down the road had had their eyes on the bungalow for years. After a quick look round and no questions, they offered the asking price. The sale went through without a hitch. Like us, the buyers didn't bother with a full survey. I would never make that mistake again. Our sigh of relief must have been audible for miles. Let the buyer beware – how true! We didn't lie, but we still felt guilty for not disclosing the faults.

***

Our next house was a three-bedroom semi in the nearby village of Breadsall. It was even closer to the college. Situated in Rectory Lane, we were just around the corner from the vicarage.

The day we moved in couldn't have got off to a worse start. Within an hour, the doorbell rang. Standing outside was a tall, angular-featured, grey-haired man in his early fifties, wearing a dog collar.

'Hello, I'm Philip Crowe from the vicarage,' announced His Reverence.

By the sour look on his face, I guessed he hadn't come for a cup of tea whilst he welcomed us to his flock.

His flock was the cause of his displeasure, or rather his diminished flock.

'Do you own a Jack Russell? Do you know where it is?'

'Yes, I think it's in the back garden. Why?'

'Because a dog, possibly your dog, got into my hen run and had one of my hens.'

Panic set in as we searched for Gyp. She had got out of the garden. As a result, one of the vicar's tasty birds had been reduced to feathers. Eventually, she came home replete, with her tail between her legs. Next day, we replaced the devoured hen.

The vicar had a field next to the vicarage where he kept sheep as well as hens. Through their love of animals, it wasn't long before Philip and Ingrid became friends.

Ingrid yearned for a few acres of land where she could indulge her passion for horses and other livestock. Fortunately, before long, her mother sold her old farmhouse and moved somewhere smaller. This enabled her to give each of her three children £10,000. This money was used to buy a 3-acre field which, by great good fortune, had come up for sale opposite our house. It was soon home to a stable block, two horses, a few sheep and a couple of pigs.

Our domestic life, or so I thought at the time, was sheer bliss. Our relationship was solid. We had two lovely daughters, a good house in an attractive village plus a 3-acre field.

At the same time I was enjoying great success in my work. In four years the number of horticultural courses had gone from four to twenty-three. As well as the main centre near Derby, we were running courses at Buxton and Chesterfield. Teaching staff had increased from four to eighteen. I had successfully applied for consent to run the college's first full-time residential course in horticulture. This growth had facilitated the go-ahead for investment in new glasshouses, polythene tunnels, an irrigation system, a plant nursery, a plant sales area, a new teaching workshop and additional decorative features. Revenue from the plant nursery was running at around £30,000 a year. Praise was lavished on me by the governing body, especially the chairman, Stan Mellors. During the Annual Awards Ceremony, whilst giving his speech to the assembled students and parents, Stan revealed that the college was to be renamed the Derbyshire College of Agriculture and Horticulture.

During refreshments afterwards, Charles Binham, his eyes sparkling, marched up to me, almost shook my arm off and said, 'I am so pleased the day has arrived when horticulture is getting the recognition and investment it deserves. The problem is as I see it, it won't be long before you up sticks and get yourself a principal's job.'

I was buzzing and felt life held no barriers for me.

I didn't see it coming, but it wasn't long before my world collapsed.

Thirteen

Tough Times and Transformations

After three or four years when nothing went wrong, I was riding the crest of my career wave. I could envisage only more success and the continuation of our happy family life. It wasn't long before it all fell to pieces. For weeks, the relationship between myself and Ingrid had become increasingly strained. She was spending less and less time at home. I didn't know why. We weren't talking. I knew something was seriously wrong, but I didn't have the confidence to broach the subject. I was afraid – afraid of finding out the truth. The atmosphere in the house was building like a volcano about to erupt.

Finally, one night, with the children asleep, I challenged her. 'Who is he then? Come on, who?'

'There's no one else. I just need my own space.'

'Oh yes! The usual stuff that's trotted out. Who is it, for God's sake?'

'There's nobody, I just said. I'm moving out.'

'When? Where to?'

'Soon. I'll be in touch.'

'What about Rachel and Laura?'

'I'm taking them with me. They need their mam.'

Within days, Ingrid and the girls had moved out. They moved into a flat in a suburb of Derby. My mental state was riddled with anguish and sorrow. I had no means or even desire to cope.

The worst time was at night. I missed the girls like crazy. Putting them to bed and reading to them at bedtime. That's when it hit me the hardest. I was miserable stuck alone in the house. 'Why? Why? Why?' went over and over in my head. I knew we probably didn't marry for the right reasons. However, I had grown extremely fond of Ingrid. Whatever love is, I believed that was what I felt for her. I mistakenly thought she felt the same about me.

Surely we could sort this out. It must be reconcilable. Maybe I had become obsessed with work and not spent enough time with her or given her sufficient attention. I suggested we try Marriage Guidance (Relate as it was called). Ingrid refused to consider this.

'There is no point. I want a divorce. Don't you understand? I don't love you. I never have.'

'But we always got on so well.'

'I know and I really liked you and I still do. But it's not enough for me, I want more.'

I couldn't accept the truth. For the next three years, I endured a most miserable time. On countless times, I was told 'Time's a great healer.' It was no consolation, even though eventually it proved to be so. In any case, I didn't want time; I wanted things back the way they were immediately. I wanted what was never going to happen.

Despite all the upheaval and my emotional turmoil, the children were our priority. They always stayed with me from Friday night to Sunday evening and as they got older for part of the school holidays.

As always, their mother remained calm and practical. Although I couldn't understand it at the time, I eventually accepted that it must have been a difficult and brave decision which Ingrid took. Had we stayed together, she would have been locked in a relationship which long-term would have been much more damaging to the family. The divorce proceeded smoothly. She had no desire to ruin me financially. I kept the house, which I soon sold and moved into a smaller, cheaper one. She kept the field.

The divorce was finalised in the summer of 1986. For the next thirty months, I lived a sad life. I was full of my own hard-done-by sorrow. Nothing seemed important any longer. At work, I wasn't fully engaged. I was freewheeling. My life was in neutral with no destination in mind. I blamed my infatuation with my career as a major factor in my marriage breakdown. In reality, I knew it wasn't the case, but it somehow made it easier to accept than the truth.

***

Peter Smith, one of the lecturers in my department, did his best to get me out of my woes. He would take me out for a drink, or to play snooker or table tennis. Most importantly, he just listened to my self-indulgent moaning and sympathised. He was a good friend and, even though we haven't seen each other for years, I will never forget his patience and kindness.

I needed a major change to get me out of this deep depression. This change, as is often the case, arrived unexpectedly. A Council Works department manager called Wesley Thorton visited Broomfield College regularly. One day, he asked me if I did any private advisory work.

'Well, I haven't, but what did you have in mind, Wesley?'

'This neighbour of mine has a two-and-a-half-acre garden. He's looking for some advice and help with the work. He owns three old people's homes so he's got a few bob!'

'Oh, that sounds pretty good. Can you fix up a meeting with him? What did you say his name is?'

Two weeks later, I was walking round Graham Sheperson's garden. It was all at the back of the house, totally hidden from the road. There was a good balance between hard and soft landscape features. Some established trees created a mild, calm microclimate. This was a garden where plants would thrive. It just needed more of them. Many more of the right kind in the right places.

'The first thing I want is to create a large mostly heather and conifer collection on the bank over there,' he said, pointing out the location. 'As you see, there are a couple of trees and a few shrubs which we would like to keep.'

'Okay, let's have a closer look. Do you know what the soil pH is?'

'No! Is that important?'

'Yes, but judging by those healthy rhododendrons next door, it's almost certainly acidic. Just to be sure, I'll test it before we decide which types of heathers to plant.'

'Well, Wesley said you were the man for the job. Can you work out how many plants it will take and how much it will cost for plants and labour?'

'Sure – I will come back, take some measurements, test the soil, calculate the number of plants and give you a price. It will take me about seven days.'

I knew I could get all the plants from the college nursery at wholesale prices. We had built up a wide range of heathers and conifers so this was indeed fortunate. With a job this size, I would need help. This was when I turned to Peter Smith, who was happy to earn a bit extra over two weekends. So I set to work on the plan and priced the job.

It came to around £1,100. To my delight, Mr Sheperson readily agreed to go ahead.

Over two dull November weekends, the transformation was complete. We were tidying up and cleaning our tools when the delighted customer approached us holding out a brown envelope.

As soon as our benefactor was out of sight, I opened the envelope. After taking off the cost of plants and materials such as fertiliser and compost, I handed Peter his share of the profit. Over the next twelve months we returned several times, on each occasion implementing new planting schemes. Graham was delighted with the transformation. Peter and I both enjoyed the creative experience and the lucrative end product.

I had found my new beginning. It was time to leave education behind and set up a landscape business. I would get back control of my life. My ambition was rekindled. It seemed so easy. All I had to do was resign. I couldn't regain my desire or commitment for my position at the college. But did I have the confidence to risk making such a major change? No! – That would take considerably longer.

Visiting the pub became a nightly event. I soon got in with the regulars at the nearby Windmill and the Rose and Crown three miles away at Morley. It was at the latter where I first met Graham Workman. He quickly spotted me and wheedled his way into my life. I was soon persuaded to help as a marshal in a fun run he was organising for a local charity. All I had to do was stand at a crossroads and point the runners the right way. Afterwards, we would meet up at the Rose and Crown for a few pints. This led to a friendship which lasted for the remainder of my time in Derbyshire.

Thanks to Graham, my recovery gained momentum. He was a boastful extrovert whose sporting prowess was only matched by his success with women, or so he would have you believe. He boosted my confidence and persuaded me to go skiing as part of a group of thirty in the winter of 1987. A fantastic time was had by all. The following year, another trip was planned for late December 1988. I was unable to go. Sadly, my father, who was in a nursing home in Kirkby Stephen, died on 4th December aged eighty. Fortunately, I had visited him only a week earlier. His funeral took placed in St Luke's Church, Soulby. He was buried in Soulby Cemetery and a funeral tea held in the village hall, formerly the primary school.

***

Spring 1989 was a defining period in my life. I decided it was time to encompass change, to tackle the fear of the unknown and to resign from the college. After several aborted attempts, I finally picked up the courage to knock on Ernie Bathurst's office door.

Once I was inside, he looked at me knowingly and asked, 'Are you all right, fella? You better sit down.'

'I am going to resign, Mr Bathurst.'

'Can't say I'm surprised, with everything that has happened. What with the divorce and recently the death of your father. Still, it's probably best for you and the college. Put it in writing. You will have to give three months' notice.' I walked out of his office thinking, *What the hell have I just done?*

***

During the summer of 1989, I set about planning my business with a lot of enthusiasm and even more trepidation. I had thrown away my safety net. The regular monthly salary would be no more. What if the business didn't generate enough profit? How would I pay the mortgage? How would I pay the monthly bills?

The fact that I knew nothing about running a business hit me head-on. Panic followed relentlessly. Help was

Rachel and Laura at Black Rock, near Cromford, in 1988 – one of their favourite walks

needed urgently. I signed up for a government-sponsored course aimed at new start-up firms like mine. Our group of eight included a boat builder, a hairdresser and a shopfitter. We absorbed every word, every tip which flowed from the tutors' all-knowing mouths. Success would surely follow, or so we all thought.

Firstly, any company needed a good name. I settled on "Hortensis". I felt it gave it a classy, distinctive-sounding air and would attract customers who were looking for a knowledgeable and professional gardener. They would, I hoped, be prepared to pay a realistic price for the service I was to provide. Secondly, I decided the business would provide the full package; namely garden design, garden construction and maintenance. My company would cover Southern Derbyshire bordering onto Nottinghamshire.

Basic hand tools and small equipment would be bought. Armed with a list, I invested in spades, forks, shovels, rakes, trowels, pruners, secateurs, brushes and wheelbarrows. Financially, it made sense to rent more expensive specialised equipment such as rotavators, cement mixers, mowing machines and hedge cutters. The cost of hire would be included in the quotation for each job.

The biggest outlay would be transport. A pick-up truck came first. It had to be signwritten. Bruce, a friend from the Rose and Crown, was a professional signwriter who did an excellent job for me. He was happy with cash going straight into his pocket. Marketing involved designing, printing and distributing leaflets and business cards. Advertising was essential. This involved a few adverts in the local paper and in those days the *Yellow Pages*.

By the time I had worked my notice, I was ready. All that was needed was for the work to roll in. A few small planting and maintenance jobs kept me going for the first two or three months. Then I clinched a couple of design and construct contracts, one of which was to create the gardens for the show houses of a local builder. These developments generated more work than I could handle on my own. Peter Smith agreed to help me part time. Before long, there was enough work for us both full time. I had to pay him more than I expected or wanted to, but I knew his abilities and work ethic. Convincing him to give up his lecturing post and work for me full time took only a matter of weeks.

Within twelve months, my workforce had expanded again with the addition of Martin, a sixteen-year-old

YTS trainee from Broomfield College. He was a great lad, very polite and hardworking. I remember one particular customer. In her seventies, Mrs Manners wanted her garden to be less labour-intensive – mostly paved areas, raised beds and a few low-maintenance plants such as low-growing conifers. This was Martin's idea of the perfect garden. He loved landscape construction. Unfortunately, from my point of view, he had no interest in plants. I brought in Ron, a self-employed bricklayer to do the skilled building work. Martin was in his element helping Ron. Mrs Manners looked after Martin like a grandson. He got far more attention than Peter or I. She would welcome us in the morning and when it was sunny her comments were always addressed to Martin.

'Hello, Martin. It's a golden morning. You bring the sun with you.'

At morning coffee and afternoon tea breaks, we were always given delicious home-made cakes or scones.

'I've got a lovely cherry cake for you today.' Her bright eyes twinkled as she looked fondly at Martin.

The jobs continued to come in. We were always busy. Very often, I was too busy. The phone would ring any day and any time of day.

I needed help with the accounts. Fortunately, a young lady called Alison who lived across the street was a trained accountant. She agreed to do my books once a fortnight. She soon advised me that the turnover had reached a point where I needed to register for VAT. This would mean much more paperwork and visits to scrutinise the accounts by the VAT inspectors (the Gestapo as they were known, and not without good reason). Well! I thought there must be a downside to all this success. VAT proved to be just one of several.

Getting work was always easier than getting paid. Most domestic customers would agree to pay a percentage for the plants and labour upfront. Commercial firms would always delay payment as long as they were legally allowed, which was up to sixty days.

Being weather-dependent, harsh winter weather created additional problems. Jobs came to a halt in severe frost or snow. This meant no invoices could be sent and no money coming in until the work was completed. Often, plants and materials had already been purchased and paid for. Steady cash flow is vital to the small business.

These uncertainties led to frequent times of euphoria alternating with depression. Two of the worst instances of the latter came in the winter of 1990/91.

***

'Dad! What's happening?'

'We're sliding – sideways!'

The people carrier juddered to a stop against a crash barrier at the edge of the road.

'Sit still, everyone! Don't jump about!'

We were teetering above a precipice. A low metal fence was all that was stopping us toppling over and ending up in the bottom of a deep ravine. My head was pulsating. But I knew I had to try and remain calm. Four children and another adult were relying on me to deliver us to safety.

It was 22nd December 1990. We were high in the French Alps, not far from our destination – the village of St Gervais, near Chamonix. Christmas was going to be a skiing holiday for me; my daughters Rachel aged nine, Laura six; Maggie my girlfriend and her girls Carol and Susan.

We had left Derby that morning amidst much jollity. The girls were singing along to a double tape of Elton John's greatest hits. They loved travelling in the cavernous Space Cruiser with its sunroof and moonroof.

Fine, sunny weather turned to heavy rain as we crossed France. As the altitude increased, snow began to fall. I stopped the car, tried to fit snow chains but failed. Yes, I should have practised before leaving home. Hindsight and all that. More snow fell as we reached higher ground. Traction diminished before the unexpected skid whilst I negotiated a sharp bend in the road.

Before long, a snow plough came hurtling up the mountain. Great! Rescue, we thought. No! It sped past. What could we do? In desperation, I put the car floor mats under the wheels. I started the engine, put it into gear and slowly released the clutch. Incredibly, the vehicle crept forward and we inched away from the barrier. There wasn't far to go, but could we make it? With immense relief, we came to the village of St Gervais. It was in darkness. In the headlights, we could see a small hotel. 'Why don't we ask here? Maybe they will let us stay the night,' suggested Maggie. 'We can find our chalet tomorrow.'

'Okay, you and the kids go inside and ask. I'll just check the car's all right. Won't be long.'

Thankfully, they found us a room. Giving us two torches, the manager explained that the severe storm had caused a power failure, but there was hot water. *Great*, I thought, *I can have a bath.* After messing about with the car mats, I was frozen. Foolishly, I jumped straight into hot water. I yelled with pain. Chilblains were, according to Maggie, an ex-nurse, the cause of my agony.

Next morning, Maggie and I were reliving our close encounter with the Grim Reaper. The girls fortunately hadn't realised how close to catastrophe we had been. Rachel had even taken photographs when our plight was at its most perilous.

After breakfast, we found our apartment. It was beautiful, with all the facilities we needed and very close to the slopes.

That afternoon, we got kitted out with skis and appropriate clothing. The nursery slopes beckoned. I had skied before. So although by no means an expert, I took the lead. Maggie and her girls could barely stay upright. Physical flexibility wasn't a natural attribute for them. Rachel soon got the hang of it. Laura looked as if she had been born in the Alps. Showing no fear, she went speeding past me – her face a picture of excited pleasure.

The rest of the week passed pleasantly enough. On Boxing Day, we drove through the Mont Blanc Tunnel into Italy and on to Switzerland. After walking the spotlessly clean streets of Geneva, we returned to our ski lodge.

The journey home began with a ten-hour drive to Calais. Maggie was in charge of navigation. We made good time until we hit the outskirts of Paris. Using the ring road, we should have skirted round the city. At the crucial time, Maggie fell asleep. We missed a vital road sign.

'All you had to do was read the bloody signs. You couldn't even do that. I've been driving for nine hours without a break.'

'Sorry, I just nodded off for a second,' she mumbled, her bottom lip quivering.

'Brilliant timing. The one and only thing you had to do.'

The outcome of this lack of concentration was three times round the Arc de Triomphe at 10 pm on a Saturday night. By the time we had found the correct road and reached the terminal, it was too late. The ferry had sailed. We booked into a hotel for the night.

This incurred further expense which I could have done without. Severe winter weather in England meant I had several unfinished landscape jobs. Until they were completed, the invoices wouldn't be sent. The holiday had already been paid for, which meant an unexpected gap in my finances.

***

Two months later, all my work came to an abrupt halt. Four or five inches of pristine white snow fell overnight. Normally, this would have been headline news, but in February 1991 the world's media was focussed on Iraq. The Gulf War had entered the combat stage. It was the first time that Exocet missiles had been seen in real time, on television – hunting down their targets. But the children were enjoying making snowmen and having snowball fights.

'Can we buy a sledge and go sledging, Dad?' asked Rachel.

'Yes please, Dad,' chirped up her sister.

'Okay, I'll see if Maggie and her girls want to come with us.'

Susan didn't like going far from the television and Carol was an avid reader. Reluctantly, they agreed to join us. That was fortunate as we could share their sledge. It hadn't seen much use anyway.

It was a sunny Saturday afternoon and we parked the car in the car park of Allestree Park on the edge of Derby.

Heading into the sun with Laura in front, between my legs, we went careering down the hill, laughing like crazy. Then we hit a patch of fine powder snow. It blew up into my eyes. I could see nothing. Still chortling, we continued our journey with our eyes closed. We came to a sudden halt. I heard a crack and felt pain coming from my right ankle.

'What's happened, Dad?'

I opened my eyes to discover we had collided with the only group of trees in that part of the park.

'We crashed into a tree. Are you okay?'

'Yes, I'm fine. Are you all right?'

'My ankle hurts a bit, but it's not too bad.'

I hobbled back to the car and drove everyone home.

Next day, Maggie nagged so much that I agreed to go to hospital. 'It looks to me as if it's broken. It needs X-raying. Get in my car now. I'm taking you to DRI' (Derbyshire Royal Infirmary).

Once there, I was ignored for hours. My temper slowly reached boiling point. I parked myself in the wheelchair provided in the middle of the corridor until I was seen. Eventually, I was taken for an X-ray. The news wasn't good. Sure enough, the ankle was broken, but to compound the problem, the ligaments were torn in three places. I would have to stay in hospital overnight and have an operation the next day.

Prior to the operation, I was told I would be given an anaesthetic. The nurse delivering this information thought for some reason that it was a good idea to tell me that the anaesthetist was an Iraqi. *My God!* I thought, *what if he wants to take revenge for Britain waging war in his country?* An overdose would reduce the enemy by one.

Back on the ward, I found my leg in plaster up to the knee. It was to stay on for eight weeks. Regular physio sessions were advised. I went to a couple. I was desperate to get the plaster off and return to work.

During this time, Peter did all the work and kept the business ticking over. The winter of 1990/91 brought home the hard realities of running a small weather-dependent business. I would have to think up some contingency plans for keeping the cash flowing when the elements connived to thwart progress in future.

***

The summer of 1991 brought a surprise development. During my time at college, I was familiar with a group called the Derby Growers. They consisted of about twenty local nursery/garden centre owners. Aubrey Harriman was one of them who owned a small ornamental nursery growing bedding plants and flowering pot plants. He was ready to retire, but didn't want to sell up until he had been granted planning permission for a small housing development.

Aubrey contacted me to ask if I fancied running the business. He didn't want any rent. However, he didn't want any major changes making. I could grow the crops he grew in the old greenhouses. He and his wife lived in a bungalow at the front of the site. He would, as he put it, be on hand to offer advice when I needed it.

It was a ramshackle set-up, but as no outlay was involved, I accepted his offer. The business training course I had attended put great emphasis on the need to diversify. Plant sales would help level out the cash flow. After last winter's financial strife, this had to be worth a gamble. Anyway, I loved raising new plants.

Running the nursery added considerably to my already heavy workload. It was a seven-day-week job: watering, feeding and controlling pests and diseases. *Cyclamen persicum* (florist's cyclamen) were grown in the greenhouses for sale around Christmas time. They needed regular fungicidal sprays to control botrytis (grey mould), a destructive fluffy mould which grows on leaves, stems and flowers.

Aubrey told me he had a supply of chemicals in his bungalow.

'You may as well have them. I won't need them anymore. Come in, we'll have a cup of tea and I'll get you something for the botrytis.'

Whilst making the tea, his wife told me Aubrey hadn't been feeling too good recently.

'Headaches and dizziness. Good job he's handed over to you.'

'Thought I hadn't seen much of him these last couple of weeks. Where's he gone now?'

'To get you that chemical from under the bed.'

'What – how long has it been there?'

'Oh, he's always kept it under the bed.'

'No wonder he doesn't feel well. He's probably poisoning himself. How do you feel, Christine?'

'Not so bad for my age, a bit shaky some days.

I told them to get rid of all the old chemicals through the council's disposal system. I would buy what I needed and keep it safe and secure. I very much doubted if they followed my advice to safely get rid of the leaking old chemical containers. They couldn't bear to waste anything.

Most of the top-quality cyclamen plants I produced were sold at Derby's wholesale market. This meant delivering them at 5.30 am. The price received was barely worth getting out of bed for. It was a similar story with all the plants I grew. The profit margin per plant was tiny. I reckoned running a nursery to be a bit like owning a biscuit factory. To make a decent living, you would have to go down the path of streamlined mass production. There were of course two major differences – biscuits didn't suffer from pests and diseases and biscuits didn't die.

By the spring of 1992, I had had enough. Landscaping was hard physical work. I didn't want to be lifting paving slabs in ten years' time. Running a small general nursery was pleasant enough, but it didn't generate enough profit.

***

A return to education with a guaranteed regular salary and those long holidays looked far more attractive than it did when I left three years ago.

I searched the job vacancies in *Horticulture Week* for about a month. At first nothing, then I found an advertisement for a position of lecturer in horticulture at Hadlow College in Kent. I was given an interview. Although disappointed not to get the job, I wasn't devastated. It was too far from the girls and awkward to get to. A couple of weeks later, I applied for the post of lecturer in horticulture at the Cambridgeshire College of Agriculture.

On a sunny morning, I set off to Milton, just outside Cambridge, for my interview. As I drove across the Fens, I was stricken by its vastness and bleakness – there were a few lonely trees, massive flat fields and no hills.

When I drove into the college, the smallness of the campus was totally unexpected. All the agricultural colleges I had known to date had an old building (often a hall) as a centrepiece, surrounded by sprawling farm buildings and hundreds of acres of farmland. This set-up consisted of two small L-shaped brick buildings and several Portakabins squeezed in behind. The grounds surrounding the buildings had been attractively landscaped, but there was scope for improvement.

I wasn't bursting with enthusiasm when I introduced myself at reception, nor was I prepared for the warmth of my welcome. During my interview, John Whittington the principal was flanked by John Clark the Chairman of Governors and Richard Walpole, a horticulturalist and Head of the Wisbech centre. I was immediately put at ease. There were no trick questions. They spoke to me as an equal. The warmth of the place and the staff when Richard showed me around was most heartening. Well, I thought, it may be small, but this is an example of something good in a small bundle.

An hour after the interview, I was called back to the principal's office and offered the job. I was delighted and relieved to accept.

Fourteen

On the Move Again

It only took one hour and fifteen minutes from Derby to my new place of work on the outskirts of Cambridge. For the first three weeks, I stayed in bed and breakfast from Monday night to Friday morning and travelled home for the weekends. My house in Derby was on the market and sold quickly.

Then I rented a two-bedroom semi in the Fenland village of Burwell, near Newmarket. It was one of about thirty identical properties built on the site of an old school. During my short time in this house, I experienced two spooky occurrences. By far the most unnerving involved several of the kitchen tiles flying off the wall and smattering on the floor. The agent arranged for a builder to carry out repairs and retile where necessary. According to the workman, the tiles had come off because when the house was built, the kitchen had been tiled before the plaster was completely dry, so they hadn't adhered to the wall as firmly as they should have. It was a plausible explanation, but I still preferred mine, which laid the blame squarely at the hands of a poltergeist. About the same time, a couple of tins of baked beans disappeared from the kitchen cupboard never to be seen again. There were some strange happenings in the Fens. No wonder they still believed in witchcraft.

This was, and still is, arable land cropped with wheat, sugar beet, potatoes and carrots. I wasn't sure if I would settle in this part of East Anglia. It looked and felt like another country, not like the England I knew. The flatness seemed to stretch forever. The Essex countryside I remembered from my college days was at least undulating, and the towns and villages possessed many attractive buildings, including churches and houses. Being virtually devoid of grassland meant very few farm animals were kept in the Fens. The bleak, flat fields were punctuated by industrial-style warehouses for root crops such as sugar beet, potatoes and carrots; the vertical towers of grain silos burst the horizontal landscape like spaceships preparing to launch.

Formed over thousands of years, the peaty soil is full of nutrients. During the late 15th and early 16th centuries, attempts were made to drain this marshy land. In 1630, some wealthy landowners hired the Dutch engineer Cornelius Vermuyden to design a drainage system using drains and wind-powered pumps. Once reclaimed from the sea, the land was superb for growing vegetables.

Driving along the straight Fen roads has its own dangers. As the peat dried out, it shrunk, resulting in the farmland being below the roads. Listing farmhouses with sunken foundations and cracks in the walls had been abandoned. The ground under the roads continued to shrink, albeit unevenly. This resulted in undulating road surfaces. The effect was akin to driving over corrugated roofing sheets – drive too quickly and you could easily achieve take-off.

Large drains (rivers) run alongside many roads. In icy conditions, the local paper often printed pictures and stories of vehicles which had slid into the notorious 40-foot drain, often with fatal consequences. During harvest time, large tractors pulling massive trailers snarled up the roads as they brought in crops. They took great delight in frustrating car drivers by hogging more of the road than they needed and refusing to pull into lay-bys to relieve the congestion behind.

The local people were hefted and couldn't envisage living anywhere else. They loved living under the massive, cloudless blue skies. Hilly northern areas were too claustrophobic and it always rained on the rare occasions they ventured above the Wash.

The people of the Fens are perhaps more inbred than in any other part of England. Before the land was drained, the many small islands were isolated. Movement was severely restricted; because of this, the gene pool remained small. On many occasions, I was told that Fen folk believed in, and some still practised, witchcraft. I never saw any evidence of this. Mind, I didn't go out of my way to seek it out.

***

I was based at Milton. It was originally the Francis Jeeps Institute and known as the Farm School. Francis Jeeps was a fruit farmer from nearby Willingham. His son Dickie was captain of the England rugby team and achieved much more fame than his father.

Milton was the smaller of the two centres surrounded on all sides by roads. There was no residential accommodation, so all the students travelled to classes daily. Every inch of land was utilised; it had to be. There was no room to expand.

Cambridge was encroaching rapidly with new bypass roads, housing estates, a Tesco supermarket and a Science Park. Computers and related technology was replacing living off the land. Courses in agriculture, horticulture, floristry, equine studies and the care of small animals were held on this compact site. Part of the library was turned over to a computer suite. All courses were taught the fundamentals needed to operate these modern contraptions.

There were only a few purpose-built brick buildings. Portakabins were used as offices. I shared with Peter Benedix, an enthusiastic and very knowledgeable agriculturalist and botanist. Before turning to lecturing, Peter had been a scientific officer for PBI (Pan Britannica

Industries, which was part of the Unilver corporation). One summer evening, Peter organised a staff outing to the PBI trial grounds just outside Cambridge. The focus of the visit was the different cultivars of wheat being bred to assess their properties for use in the making of beer. As interesting as it was to discover which qualities were being assessed and why, the best was saved to last.

Peter wondered, 'Would you like to sample a few bottles made from the varieties being tested and give your opinions on the tastiest?'

'Of course,' we all said in unison. 'We thought you would never ask.'

The compact gardens which enveloped the college buildings had been attractively planted with a wide range of trees, shrubs and herbaceous perennials. I was given free rein by the principal and the head of centre to do what I thought needed doing, provided the fortnightly centre management group agreed with my plans. This suited me just fine. Everyone was very supportive of my ideas and delighted to see the improvements as they took shape. All the new features, including a hedge around the perimeter and a pergola leading to a herb garden, were an integral part of the students' practical training.

The larger of the two glasshouses was empty when I took up my post. In the past, it had produced crops of tomatoes. This was no longer financially viable. A change of use to ornamental plants was needed. The structure would then provide a relevant practical facility for the students we hoped to recruit from the amenity sector, such as parks departments and ornamental nurseries.

The first job was to remove all the top soil (it was spread on the outside beds). A mini digger was hired to excavate the soil. It was delivered early one morning. The lorry driver got back into his cab. 'Aren't you staying to drive it?' I shouted as he was about to leave.

'No mate, not me.'

'Well, who is then?'

He looked at his paperwork. 'No driver booked, one of you will have to use it. It's easy. Just a mini digger,' were his parting words.

Panic-stricken, I looked at Richard, the technician. Now Richard was a steady worker who had been transferred from the college's Wisbech centre to work with me. His flexibility, like his skills, was limited. Neither of us had driven a mini digger before, let alone within the confines of a glasshouse.

'No, I'm not doing it. I'll watch and guide you, though.'

'Tell you what, Richard, I'll practise a bit outside first.'

'Okay, good luck. Keep away from those cars.'

He always knew how to instil confidence.

I soon got the hang of the controls before venturing inside. All was going well. Then I got too cocky and the bucket veered towards the glass. My attempts at corrective action were a fraction too late. Two large panes of glass shattered into small fragments. Cursing and embarrassed, I stepped down from the machine to a round of applause from the small group of staff assembled on the lawn. Richard, bless him, had replaced dozens, if not hundreds, of panes of glass during his career as a glasshouse technician.

From then on, the transformation to a pot-plant glasshouse was trouble-free.

Most practical classes went without a hitch, but I recall one which caused me and some students much distress. On a hot, sunny day, we had been pruning the herb rue (*Ruta graveolens*). We should have worn gloves, because the sap from this herb can cause a very irritating rash. This time it did and my skin erupted. I went to the village doctors who diagnosed that the rash resulted from plant sap. He didn't know which plant but prescribed calamine lotion.

'Nothing to worry about, that'll soon clear it up. Have you still got pigs at the farm school?'

'Yes, doctor, thank you. Where do I get this lotion?'

'Tesco's chemists will have it. I'll write the name down. It doesn't cost much.'

The next day, two students reported the same problem. I put them onto the calamine lotion.

I don't think it helped one jot, because it took about three weeks to clear up. During this time, I worried that the affected students would take legal action for my negligence. Fortunately, my worries were unfounded.

During my teaching career, I always relished the challenge of introducing new courses. In Cambridgeshire, there were an increasing number of golf courses. Trainee greenkeepers had to travel out of the county to gain qualifications. After identifying this gap in the market, I put together a City and Guilds course, getting the support of the industry and creating on a hitherto empty plot of college land some basic practical facilities for golf course management.

Recruitment to the greenkeeping courses exceeded expectations. Numbers soon meant the need for another member of teaching staff based with me at Milton.

A steering committee was established consisting of two head greenkeepers, myself and the new lecturer. We met once a month at 7.30 pm. Tea, coffee and biscuits were funded from the petty cash tin which the principal kept in his desk. I bought the essential ingredients from Tesco. After the meeting, I was responsible for washing up the crockery. Unlike any of the previous colleges I had worked in, there was no need for kitchen staff, because there was no kitchen.

***

On Mondays, I taught at the Wisbech centre, which was close to the borders of Cambridgeshire, Norfolk and Lincolnshire. Before it became part of the Cambridgeshire College of Agriculture and Horticulture, it was the Horticultural Station of the Isle of Ely. Thirty-five miles north of Milton, it was an hour's drive across the Fens, the only notable landmark being the magnificent Ely Cathedral sitting on an area of raised ground. This stunning building deserves its description as the ship of the Fens. Areas of habitation were few, with unimaginative names such as Upwell and Outwell. The vast blue skies were indeed splendid, without which the monotonous landscape would have been unbearable.

The college entrance, reception area and offices desperately needed an upgrade. There was a large block of relatively modern glasshouses. They were not producing the quantity and range of commercial crops such as tomatoes, cucumbers and peppers they did when the unit was in its most viable period. Local growers couldn't compete with cheap, all-year-round imports from countries such as Spain and the Netherlands. Student recruitment was low. The same fate had befallen the fruit industry. Uneconomic orchards had been cleared. The Wisbech centre retained only a few acres of apples and pears. Consequently, student recruitment had shrunk. The college was trying to counteract this decline by diversifying. Like the Milton centre, they provided courses in equine studies, small animal care and environmental studies. Horticulture was moving further into the amenity sector. Despite considerable time and effort spent on recruitment, most of the Fen farmers were of the opinion that they could teach their children all they needed to know.

***

A few of the equine department staff from both centres were smitten by the diversification bug. The main mover in this development was Anne Ratcliff, the Head of Equine Studies. She was convinced that the way to vast riches and her escape from the daily grind was through the American organisation called Amway. She persuaded me to give it a try. The company put its name to cleaning products. Although not officially a pyramid-selling organisation, the participants' success or otherwise depended on attracting new recruits to the organisation.

Anne took me to two Amway meetings. Designed to whip up enthusiasm amongst the members, they were what I imagined an American Evangelist extravaganza would be like. The inspirational guest speakers entered the room to loud rock music (Tina Turner blasting out *Simply the Best*, etc). At this point, the orchestrated gathering stood on their chairs, whooping and frantically waving above their heads the mind-manipulating papers which all the delegates received as they entered the building. Once back home, we would all, with unwavering conviction, persuade many more members to sign up to the Amway crusade. I tried, not, I must admit, wholeheartedly, to convince a few of my neighbours to join. I had no success at all. It wasn't for me.

***

At the Wisbech centre, my role was to teach decorative horticulture. Theory was covered in the morning in the well-equipped, purpose-built teaching block. Afternoons were devoted to practicals. Most of the amenity areas were ripe for a makeover. Plants loved the peaty soil, where broken-off shoots of plants would readily form roots, and seeds germinated, like mustard and cress.

A new pond, new perennials and tree and shrub areas were established around the buildings. Before too long, the site looked as if it belonged to someone.

Richard Walpole, a highly qualified horticulturalist, was head of the Wisbech centre. He was also responsible for land-based adult education evening classes throughout

Cambridgeshire. My duties included the delivery of gardening classes in the Cambridge area.

The college maintained links with the Cambridge Botanic Garden. Student visits to the Botanics were included in the syllabus for horticultural courses. I was always convinced that these ties should be strengthened and that the two organisations should join forces to market and deliver a course which would have wider appeal than the ones offered solely by the college.

After eighteen months, I felt very settled in Cambridgeshire. I had become accustomed to the flat landscape, and the appeal of the large blue skies was growing on me. What's more, it didn't rain very much. But, perhaps more than anything else, I loved the job. There was very little pressure. I was part of an extremely friendly, happy and supportive small band of staff. I decided it was time to stop throwing money away on renting and to buy a house.

Before for too long, I opted for a two-bedroom semi in the village of Papworth Everard, about 10 miles to the west of Cambridge. It was just around the corner from Papworth Hospital, renowned for its ground-breaking work on heart transplants.

The houses I had rented had both been furnished, so all my possessions were easily transported in my people carrier. I moved into 13 Dengaine Close in October 1993. Me and my dog of mixed breeds, who answered to the name of Nipper.

***

Life was good in 1993 but there was something missing in my life. Apart from Nipper, I had no one to share it with on a daily basis. I saw Rachel and Laura regularly, but I hadn't been in a relationship since Maggie and I went our separate ways after I left Derby.

The stumbling block was where to meet members of the opposite sex in an effort to find someone with whom you might click. A few years ago, it seemed easy to start chatting in a pub and occasionally, as with Maggie and I, we talked to each other in the Rose and Crown several times before our friendship developed into a more advanced union. The chances of a repeat at the age of forty-five seemed slim. I tried the village pub, which went by the odd name of Kisby's Hut. It was a haven for lovers of heavy metal. Trying to talk to anyone was pointless if you couldn't lip-read. Just making yourself heard when ordering a drink was nigh on impossible.

So, rather reluctantly, I resorted to reading adverts in the local evening paper. I replied to about three females with whom I thought I might have something in common. We met up, had a drink and a chat for an hour or so. In all cases, it was clear to both parties that there was no chemistry between us and we thought it best after a pleasant enough time not to pursue our efforts. Oh well, I thought, may as well try again, nothing ventured as it were. One advert struck me as being written by someone who was a bit different. After so long, I can't remember the exact wording, but it didn't contain the usual clichés and references to being honest, caring and looking for a like-minded soulmate. So I rang the number and we had a short but interesting chat. We both thought it would be worthwhile meeting for a couple of drinks. The date, time and place were set. It was to be the second Wednesday in June in the Grafton shopping centre, just outside the Albion Tavern at 7.30 pm. But just before she rang off, I suddenly thought how will I recognise her? She had told me she had long, wavy black hair. What if there were several others with similar hair in the same vicinity at the same time? 'Okay,' she exclaimed, 'I will be carrying a very colourful bag.'

We both arrived about five minutes early. The place was very quiet. Nervously, we approached each other. We both spoke at the same time. 'You must be Barbara.'

'You must be David.' Nervous laughter ensued.

'Do you fancy a drink?' I said.

'Oh, yes please,' came the reply. Minutes later, inside the Albion, we were knocking back red wines and smoking the first of many cigarettes that night. Two hours later, the ashtray was full. Closing time came around remarkably quickly. We agreed to meet again in a few days' time. Before long, we were seeing each other on a regular basis. We had clicked and it felt really good. Still, we both thought it better not to get too carried away in those early days – what will be, will be.

I had been living at Papworth for about seven months. The small garden was just as it was left by the builders – a few paving slabs outside the patio doors and the rest turf. It was time to do something with my estate. So I thrust my spade into the earth only for it to be met with resistance. I stood on the spade and pushed, yet still it barely penetrated the surface. The clay soil had baked like concrete in the arid Cambridgeshire climate. I drenched the ground where I wanted to create a border. After the water had soaked in, I was able to turn over the area bit by bit.

The garden hadn't progressed very far before I was on the move again. I had no intention of moving at that time. Barbara and I were very happy together and I had a job I enjoyed without much pressure. Then the post of Senior Lecturer/Head of Horticulture at Newton Rigg College was advertised. Since I had come to Cambridgeshire, I had always yearned to be appointed to a position at the same level as that from which I walked away in Derbyshire. As my old principal Ernie Bathurst said on more than one occasion, 'Ambition can be a cruel master.' I wasn't at all sure if I wanted to return to Cumbria, let alone work in the college where I began my training. It had until then been my belief that it was wrong to go back anywhere. After much deliberation, I sent off my application form. I was invited for interview.

Fifteen

Back to the Fells

During my student days, it was the Cumberland and Westmorland College of Agriculture and Forestry. When I went back for my interview in July 1994, it had become Newton Rigg College and was no longer part of the County Council.

What hadn't changed was the weather. It was summer, yet compared to the south of the country it was bitterly cold. The fells of the Lake District and the Pennines were still majestic. Maybe I had become soft after twenty-five years in warmer climes.

I was provided with overnight accommodation in a college hostel. It was out of term time so it was quiet. I got as good a night's sleep as possible considering my hyped-up state of mind and the low temperature.

The next morning, after a filling breakfast in the

dining room, myself and the three other candidates were given a guided tour of the college by Stephen Oliver-Watts, the Head of the School of Business and Extended Education. Horticulture was included in this amalgam of various subject areas. The grounds and gardens were now referred to as the campus. They hadn't changed much since my student days. A new students' hostel was being built and a new dining room, but farm buildings were still an integral part of the complex. The gardens and the glasshouse section looked much like they did in the late 1960s. The only new horticultural development was, as I recall, a garden design studio being created in one of the old farm buildings.

Formal interviews took place after lunch, part of which was to present a lecture of our choosing to Stephen and for some reason which none of us could fathom, to Margaret Bradbury, the Head of Human Resources. Never before had any of the applicants been asked to perform in this way as part of an interview. Even more bemusing was the fact that we never met Ken Jackson, the principal.

As revealed during the interview, the successful applicant would as part of their duties act as course manager for the Higher National Diploma in Amenity Horticulture. This was to be Newton Riggs' first higher education course in horticulture. It was to be full time over two years and had been validated by the University of Central Lancashire. I was the second candidate to be interviewed. The nerve-racking wait for the panel's decision went on and on. Finally, the successful candidate was called back to the interview room. I was told it was me and did I accept the post? I said yes, and thanked the panel for offering it to me.

That evening, I drove back to Papworth Everard elated, but still unsure if it really was what I wanted. I would have to resign tomorrow. Why was I doing this when I was happy and appreciated where I was? Barbara and I had only known each other for a few weeks, but what would become of our promising relationship if I moved to the other end of the country? How and when would I break the news to her? I would be further away from my children and most likely see less of them. I tried to convince myself that they were getting older and maybe wouldn't mind seeing less of me in future. If I changed my mind and turned down the job in Cumbria, I may never get a similar position again anywhere, let alone in the county of my birth. Cumbria won the toss.

***

On Monday, 10th October 1994, I started work at Newton Rigg College. I was to share an office with two horticultural colleagues, Antony Wills and Francis Deane. Antony, a former bank worker, had several years' service, but Francis came straight from university, having commenced her duties just two months before me. The office was part of a revamped old farm building known as the bull pen. It felt very much as if we were in a sparring contest as we got to know each other. On top of that, I had to lecture to and act as course manager for a higher education group of students. It was a first for me and I was very nervous when

I met the group of fifteen. They sensed my unease, but with a couple of exceptions they were very gentle with me.

Meeting new colleagues, finding your way around the various departments and being shown new systems is always challenging when you start at a new place of employment. After the small set-up at Cambridge, this was particularly daunting. I would have to liaise with staff of UCLAN whose headquarters were in Preston. I would have to correspond via email. This prospect filled me with dread. I would have to travel to Preston for meetings.

I soon discovered there was an obsession with computerised systems. Whether or not these methods led to improvements didn't appear to be taken into account. Timetabling was computerised and centralised. Each section had to submit its request for rooms and staff to the person who fed the information into a programme. This was very confusing and unnecessarily complicated. I could and should have been able to do it myself. All I needed was a pad of A3-sized paper, a pencil, a ruler and a couple of rooms dedicated to horticulture. There were constant glitches with timetabling, and like all the other section leaders, I wasted hours and hours trying to sort out the problems with Dorothy, whose unenviable job was to create a smooth running program.

In previous colleges where I worked, I had always enjoyed being in control of the gardens. This wasn't so at Newton Rigg. I wasn't aware when I was appointed, but several years earlier, the head gardener had been given overall control of the grounds. This meant in my opinion that they had too much say in how the practical teaching areas were managed. I felt that the head gardener should have been under the direction of the senior member of the teaching staff. Doubts regarding the wisdom of accepting the job were gaining momentum.

***

'We have been waiting for this moment for five weeks. Now at last I can introduce you to your course manager, David Haigh.'

With that brief introduction from my line manager, Stephen Oliver-Watts, I was launched into my career at Newton Rigg College. Fifteen pairs of eyes were scrutinising me intently. They belonged to the students on the college's first-ever full-time Higher National Diploma Course in Amenity Horticulture. I wanted to disappear, but there was no way out.

I had never taught full-time or higher-education students before. It was a daunting prospect. The course had started in early September and it was now mid-October. They knew their way around the campus better than me and were more familiar with the course content, the workload and the level at which they were expected to perform. I had never before heard college grounds and gardens referred to as a campus, and what for God's sake was a semester? (Turned out it was a term.) Why these American words had to be used I know not, nor why the word *module* replaced *subject*.

To add further pressure, I didn't have a home. For the first three weeks, I lived in one room in a student hostel.

Living in close proximity to a bunch of raucous beer-swilling agricultural students wasn't conducive to peaceful living. Nipper stayed with my brother, John, and his wife, Dorothy. I spent a few weekends with them at Kirkby Stephen. On some occasions, I was able to finish work early on Friday afternoon and drive down to Cambridge to stay with Barbara. Why had I given up the life I had in Cambridgeshire?

***

Gradually, I settled in. Finding a house to rent in the attractive Eden Valley village of Great Salkeld was a blissful development. It belonged to a Newton Rigg employee Pam Jago and her husband, Hugh. My furniture and belongings arrived within two weeks.

Most wonderful of all was that Nipper and I were reunited. She loved her new home in the country. We enjoyed regular walks alongside the River Eden. Chasing rabbits was a great source of excitement and exercise for her. One such escapade ended in Nipper having a near fatal accident. In pursuit of a furry bunny, she scaled a tall stone wall and scrambled down the other side, closing in on her prey. Unfortunately, a strand of barbed wire ripped a deep gash out of her undercarriage. It was early evening and I panicked. She wasn't registered with a vet. I didn't know what to do. In desperation, I bandaged her in a towel, bundled her in the car and drove as fast as I could to Kirby Stephen. Dorothy telephoned the vets in the town and they said to bring her in immediately. Thirty minutes later and with three stitches in her stomach, I collected her from the surgery.

The tough pooch showed no distress following her rabbit-hunting trauma. But she was never able to run as easily again. Too many twists and turns had caused ligament damage in her right rear leg. As she got older, she became less agile. This problem was compounded as she gained weight due to too many leftovers. Nipper would stay with John and Dorothy when I and later Barbara went away for a break. When we collected her, she had expanded considerably. Dorothy must have fed her constantly from cereal for breakfast, meat at any time (lucky dog spending holidays with a butcher) and chocolates. She thought she was being kind. Nipper never refused food.

***

At the end of my first academic year, I took the HND students on a study tour. Grants were available to fund these educational additions to the core course. I had to justify this trip as a valuable educational experience for the students. The expenses to be incurred in order to cover the costs had to be justified before approval was given. In early June, we left Newton Rigg in a college minibus destined for a selection of highly regarded gardens in the south of England. Everything went without a hitch. However, it can't have been particularly memorable. My only recollection of it now, twenty-four years later, is spending an evening in a rather down-at-heel pub in

Milton Keynes. This was followed the next day by a trip to Waddesdon Manor, which was the most memorable garden we visited. Run by the National Trust, this stately home was built for Baron de Rothschild in the 1870s. We didn't go into the house. The outside of the intricately ornate building and the adjacent parterre with its perfectly grown brightly coloured bedding plants was the finest example of extreme opulence I have seen to this day. How many plants and how much they had cost to produce and care for to provide this one-season spectacle was a topic for conversation on our way to our next destination of Blenheim Palace.

The tour was a well-deserved reward for the students. They had responded positively to my efforts to provide them with a beneficial experience during their first year on this the college's first-ever higher education in horticulture.

Their studies had culminated in the award of a gold medal and Best Large Garden at the Holker Hall Garden Festival in late May. £1,500 was spent on plants and materials. At the time, this was way over what the college was expecting to spend. Steven Oliver-Watts was very supportive and gave the go-ahead. He felt as I did that we needed to increase our profile to attract potential students, and Holker Show was at the time the most important gardening event in the north west of England. Lord and Lady Cavendish, the owners of the estate, were fanatical horticulturalists and were delighted to welcome us to the festival for the first time. The students designed, created and cared for their garden during the three days of the show. It was also the first time the college had entered such a competition, and a first for me, whose main role was to cajole and organise the group to work to a tight schedule and to a very high standard.

It was hard work for all concerned for three weeks, beginning with transporting materials there and clearing the site, returning it to the condition it was before we started and taking everything back to Newton Rigg. Worthwhile definitely, and all involved felt a great swell of pride. However, I don't recall recruiting any additional students on the back of this success. Still, successive courses repeated the involvement with equal success in the next five or six years.

***

The new intake of HND students who enrolled in September 1995 achieved more than any other in my time at Newton Rigg. A mixture of ages and abilities, the more capable encouraged the others to reach their maximum potential. This group was a pleasure to manage during their two-year course.

Assignments were always handed in on time, and every student, whatever the module, worked diligently. (This was in stark contrast to many years when students excelled in moaning about the content and delivery of some modules. Business studies were a regular target for their not-so-friendly fire.)

But it was not just their coursework that stood out above the average. No, it was their desire to experience and benefit from taking part in activities that weren't written into their course syllabus.

Two students, Debbie and Fiona, took complete control of the study tour at the end of their first year. They volunteered to organise every aspect, from deciding which gardens to visit to booking the bed and breakfast accommodation. It would, they claimed, be evidence of their organisational skills and could be used as such in one of their business modules.

Within days, their intentions were introduced to me and the rest of the group. 'We plan to visit a number of gardens in the Irish Republic,' announced Fiona.

'Here is a leaflet for you. We have marked the ones we think look the most interesting and varied,' added Debbie.

Taken aback by the speed with which they had come up with this educational extravaganza, I chuntered about the finances, asking, 'Have you any idea how much this will cost?'

'Yes, we have. It's all itemised for you. The garden entrances and the bed and breakfast accommodation,' said Fiona as she gave me one of her disarming smiles.

'What about fuel for the minibus and the cost of the ferry crossing?'

'That's down here as well,' announced a triumphant Debbie as she held aloft two sheets of A4.

'Well, you have been busy. What do the rest of you feel about such an adventure?'

They only mumbled their ascent except the vociferous Mark who as usual was very animated in his enthusiasm regarding a holiday in Ireland. 'There's nothing like the

Guinness in Dublin and the clubs in Temple Bar never close.' He delighted in delivering these gems to the younger males, like the easily led Tom.

As this juncture, I had with some difficulty to adopt my sternest expression and remind them that it was an educational study tour which was being planned and not a holiday being paid for by the college. Besides, it had to be approved by an academic sub-committee, and the organisers (Fiona and Debbie) would have to fill in an application document. They would have to justify the tour on educational grounds and list all the expenses. If approved, then all receipts must be retained and handed into the college finance office on our return. They would also be required to complete a post-tour report for the academic board.

None of this documentation bothered them one bit. Inwardly, I gave a sigh of relief whilst thinking *thank goodness I don't have to do it*. Unconditional approval was given for the tour to take place in early June at the end of the academic year.

The group had rounded off their first year by emulating last year's first-year students at the Holker Garden Festival.

On a warm, sunny Saturday morning, we loaded a college minibus with essentials and set off for the ferry terminal at Holyhead. Driving was my only duty for the next seven days. By early evening, we were on Irish soil and heading towards Enniskerry in County Wicklow to find our first night's bed and breakfast. It was an old farmhouse in the shadow of Sugarloaf Mountain. The hospitality, food and sleeping accommodation were all first class.

Next day, we travelled the short distance to our first garden, Powerscourt. This majestic creation is a mixture of formal gardens, ornamental lakes, a walled garden and a Japanese garden. For myself and most of the students, the terraces sweeping down and away from the house were the most stunning feature. From Powerscourt, we travelled south to Mount Usher – without doubt the most popular garden of the week. This natural and relaxingly informal garden was packed with a vast range of plants, from the smallest ground-hugging hardy perennials to the loftiest most venerable trees.

Ballymaloe Cookery School and Garden just outside of Cork is a must for visitors of Irish gardens. Finding it was quite a challenge. Driving in the Republic for the first time requires patience and a sense of humour, as road signs often seem to take you round in circles. But the experience when we toured Ballymaloe more than made up for the short delay. The feature which I found most remarkable (amongst many others) was the Shell House. This small building had a slate roof and gothic windows. The inside walls, window sills and ceiling were decorated with beautiful shells which had been cemented on.

The tour wasn't just about gardening. The students and I enjoyed our evenings. There was one wonderful night in Kilkenny. We were staying overnight in a pub. The accommodation and food was first class. The evening's entertainment was even better. Live music being provided by several talented acts who performed until midnight.

It was on this occasion that I learned from Fiona of my recently bestowed nickname. They thought it appropriate to call me Dad. The last night was spent in Dublin. After dinner, it was decided that we would all go to a nightclub.

'You as well, Dad,' chorused Debbie and Fiona.

'Oh no, you don't want me with you. I'd cramp your style.'

'Don't be such an old fuddy-duddy. You're coming, that's final.'

Soon we set off on the short walk to the Temple Bar area. I trudged along reluctantly.

Mark and Tom said they would look after me. Next day, I realised that what they meant was they would ply me with sufficient Guinness to loosen me up. It obviously did. They even persuaded me to get on the dance floor. The night was great fun for everyone and a great way to round off the academic year.

Debbie and Fiona were determined to get maximum benefit from their time at Newton Rigg. They were capable of coping with the demands of the course and still finding time to participate in projects that would supplement their knowledge and experience. They were winners and thrived on meeting new challenges. On the return journey from Ireland, they informed me of their latest proposal. The Royal Horticultural Society (RHS) was putting on a new event next year, near Glasgow, to be known as Scotland's National Gardening Show. The girls wanted to enter the show garden competition.

Of course, their plans were well down the line. They knew how to apply to participate. First draft plans of their proposals were almost complete. Due to financial constraints, I had to sound a few words of caution. This they had anticipated. They assured me that the cost to the college would be minimal. They were confident they could get local firms to supply or loan, where possible, plants and materials. If Newton Rigg could only provide the transport for several trips to deliver and return everything, then they reckoned that with the aid of a few fellow students it could be achieved.

Sure enough, on a cold Scottish day in late May 1997, their courtyard garden was awarded a "Silver Gilt" medal. The Princess Royal was guest of honour. She toured the site and met and chatted to all the competitors. Newton Rigg's marketing manager thought this was a great opportunity for college publicity. With camera poised, he tried to push his way in to get the ideal photo shoot. The strong hand of one of Princess Anne's bodyguards alighted upon his shoulder before a few gentle words from the security officer moved him well away from HRH.

***

Stephen Oliver-Watts called me to his office first thing on a Monday in early January 2000. I feared the worst but couldn't think what I had done wrong or not done.

'Sit down, David, and don't look so worried. I had a call from Border Television late on Friday afternoon. They have this idea regards the making of a gardening series and would like to involve our students. I expect they see it as a way of making a programme involving minimum expense. Anyway, I said you and I would go over to Carlisle and meet with Harry King, the producer. We would get a better idea of what his proposals are and how feasible it would be to take part.'

I could barely control my excitement. This would be a very welcome change from the monotonous paperwork and tedious assessments, which took up lots of my workload.

'Nothing to lose by going to see what he has in mind. It could be an extremely worthwhile experience for the students and an insight into a potential career for any with broadcasting ambitions.'

'Excellent. In that case, I will confirm with Harry that we will meet him tomorrow at 10.30 am. We'll go in my car. Let's meet here at 9.50 am.'

Harry King, a jovial little fella, came bouncing down the stairs. He had worked at Border Television since it opened its doors on 1st September 1961. Over coffee, he outlined his plans for a gardening series which he called *Dig That Plot*. 'I have this idea that it will be a garden design and construction show, in the form of a competition.'

'You say construction, Harry. What do you have in mind?' asked Steve.

'Well, we have a big area of unused land next to the car park which could be used. I will show you after coffee.'

'Yes, but where will these teams come from and what will their brief involve?' I wanted to know.

'There will be four teams, four gardeners in each team. One from each part of the Border TV region. Their gardens will have to depict the unique character of the regions they represent. I was hoping that Newton Rigg with its contacts and past students could suggest and persuade suitable team leaders and other participants for each group. In addition, I would like your students to create a special garden which could be used for filming future outdoor programmes, such as gardening and cookery.'

'It's got the makings of a fine programme, but it won't come cheap.'

'That's the rub. Money is very tight. We were hoping you could acquire plants and materials at either cost price or as donations for the television exposure.'

The site was big enough, easily accessible for vehicles and wouldn't involve too much ground preparation. My experience with the show gardens meant that I was well experienced in creating gardens on the smallest of budgets. Plus, I knew that if I could involve a few of the past students with track records of obtaining plants and materials for a song, then this project was a goer. But it would be no mean task getting together four teams with the component parts of each being able to work in harmony to a tight time schedule.

Steve and I looked at each other and nodded simultaneously. Harry grinned from ear to ear and we shook hands.

We travelled throughout Cumbria and south west Scotland filming the students as they went about the task of acquiring plants, landscape supplies and artefacts. A day was spent filming at Newton Rigg in the Design Studio and the Tropical Plant House. Harry's meticulous planning where every item and move was written down and timed to the minute ensured that it all went seamlessly. His attention to detail could at times be rather tedious. However, it was something I never forgot and was very grateful for, a few years later, in my role as a Gardens Holiday Host.

We had less than four months to make this programme. Many hours of filming ended up after editing with five thirty-minute programmes. One programme was devoted to each team and their garden, and the final programme was devoted to the students' special garden and the judging of the four competitors.

Vivien Russell, noted garden photographer, garden writer and former wife of film director Ken Russell, was one of the judges, the other being Henry Noblett, my old mentor – former Head of Horticulture at Newton Rigg and Border Television's first TV gardener, who had worked with Harry King on many occasions.

At the end of judging, Henry announced the winning garden. After praising all the entrants in time-honoured fashion and with a delay to build up the tension, he opened an envelope and proclaimed, 'The winner is the garden which represents the Settle to Carlisle Railway Line.'

'Would the team leader please step forward to collect their award,' said Harry.

I couldn't have been happier. The winning garden fitted the brief exactly and it was the brainchild of Fiona Ashford. One of the most conscientious, able and hardworking students I ever had the pleasure to teach.

The series was broadcast in early autumn. I watched the credits over and over again. Never had I expected to see my name on screen, as the "Associate Producer".

***

On a cold January morning in 2001, a familiar voice came down the line. 'David, I've got an idea for another gardening series. Involving you and your students again.'

'What are you scheming this time, Harry?'

'Well, it's forty years since Border first went on air, so I thought why not create four gardens – one for each decade? The '60s, '70s, '80s and '90s. Oh, and the larger garden which the students built last year could be modified and added to with some futuristic touches.'

'Umm, sounds like a lot of work. Difficult to justify all the time it would take. I'm not saying no, but I need to somehow incorporate aspects into a few course modules. That way, Steve might agree.'

'Okay, see what you can come up with. Come over next week for coffee and we can work it out.'

By the end of the month, we were watching the students dismantling last year's *Dig That Plot* gardens. This time, Harry thought it would be a good idea to ask the students for ideas for a title for this new series. He decided that *Bordering on Forty* fitted best.

Each team was made up of three students – a team for each decade and one for the first decade of the millennium. Designs were drawn up and scrutinised by myself for their relevance to the decade they depicted.

Following amendments, students were than tasked with obtaining plants, materials and machinery. As last year, it was a case of beg, steal or borrow. Construction and filming of the new gardens began in February. Harry spent many hours directing filming operations from a cherry picker sited in the car park. I was tasked with keeping watch over operations at ground level. I recall one Saturday afternoon when a lapse of concentration meant I missed an incident during which an operation involving machinery was filmed without the operative wearing the necessary protective clothing. When I finally realised what was happening, I waved frantically at the cameraman to stop filming.

Harry came down from his perch looking very disgruntled and demanded to know what was wrong. I explained and apologised for my lapse. It was the only time I felt the rough edge of his tongue. 'Damn it, we'll have to shoot that piece again. Stay awake in future. That's all you have to do.'

Like the last series, Harry's planning was finely tuned. If only the students had been as keen to stick to his schedule as he and I were, it would have been a much less stressful experience. If they understood, they certainly didn't appreciate the amount of time needed to edit prior to hitting deadlines so that the series would be ready for the scheduled broadcasting dates.

It was my job to find gardens throughout Cumbria which matched those which were typical of the four decades. I then obtained the permission of the owners for their gardens to be filmed. We also interviewed a number of local characters, asking them to reminisce about how their gardens and their approach to gardening had changed over the last forty years. I remember the wise words of Terry from Aspatria when describing how in his twenties he would rush into every job, 'But now, in my fifties, I sit down with a cup of tea and maybe some toast and think about it. Then I think about it a bit more, then a bit more. After that, I'll do a bit.'

Filming gardens and gardeners was most enjoyable. Sadly, every journey was dampened by horrendous sights and smells as we drove through the usually idyllic countryside. It was the year of foot-and-mouth, and images of dead sheep piled up in farm gateways and the stench of funeral pyres lingered long in the memory.

Despite everything, *Bordering on Forty* turned out to be a successful series. Sadly, the Border Television studios in Carlisle fell victim to the merger philosophy and were closed before the end of the decade.

Sixteen

Allotments and Other Good Things

'Hope you're prepared for hard work. The rewards are well worth it. But don't expect overnight success. We get a lot that do. They never last long.' Those were the wise words of Rodney, chairman of St Aidan's Allotment Society in Carlisle. He was showing us around the available plots on a mild, dull Saturday in January 2000.

Not wishing to boast or give too much away at that stage, I just said, 'Well, I've grown fruit and vegetables for many years, but the present garden isn't really big enough for us.' That seemed to satisfy his requirements, which were minimal. It was a couple of years before the allotment revival, and the committee didn't have a waiting list. There were seven plots available. Barbara and I settled for the one which needed the least work to get rid of the perennial weeds and the rubbish.

'Good choice. I would have gone for that one,' said Rodney. 'If you pile up all the rotten wood and broken glass in the far corner, the city council will collect it and take it away.' We shook hands; he wished us luck and toddled off back to his own plot at the other end of the site.

We were delighted with our new venture and couldn't wait to get started. 'Now it's important to make a plan and do the preparation in logical fashion,' I pronounced.

Allotment Jan 2000

'Okay, that's fine. Don't we get rid of the rubbish first?'

'Of course we do.'

'All right, there's no need to sound so superior. I'm not one of your students and don't need telling what to do all the time.'

After this little tiff, work progressed smoothly and relatively quickly. The rubbish was cleared. Rabbit-proof

Barbara in pond being constructed in 1997 at Gt Salkeld

David in Waterfall
at Gt Salkeld

DLH relaxing after working
on Salkeld pond

fencing was bought and erected over three days. Then followed what many would consider the laborious task of digging (as always, it was a pleasure for me, which gave deep satisfaction). The ground was infested with a wealth of couch grass and dock roots. I dug for over thirty-two hours, removing as many roots as was possible. Digging, which was completed in March, had been accompanied by many caustic and some amusing comments from other allotmenteers. The plot holder on one side, known as Killer on account of his fighting prowess (as a young man), told me, 'You want to get your taties in. You can play about with that anytime.'

Willie Bell on the other side related the tale of the dock root and the farmer. 'Old George Taylor nailed a dock root to his barn door. Two years later, he took it down and planted it. Course it grew again. You'll never get rid of them.'

'Well, maybe not all of them, but I will start with the ground as clear of them as possible.'

'Aye, well, good luck with that,' he chortled. 'I've had two plots on this site for over thirty years and so have a good many others. We haven't shifted them yet. If I were you, I would get something planted. When are you going to get your taties in?'

Picking Plums with Nipper 2004

God, I thought, *all they can think about is their bloody taties.*

The first year, the layout was in the time-honoured utilitarian method of straight rows of common vegetables, including a few rows of potatoes, peas, broad beans, cabbages, carrots, onions and leeks.

The summer of 2000 was a busy period. As well as a new allotment, I had a new house to move into and decorate. My house in Great Salkeld was tiny, and travelling to and from the allotment in Carlisle was an inconvenient chore. With Barbara's help, I moved to a three-bed semi in Stanwix, North Carlisle on 1st June. The garden was twice the size of the one in Great Salkeld. Together with the allotment, we would be able to grow many more plants. The anticipation of sowing, planting and harvesting fruit and vegetables saw us through the following winter as we planned for next year. We would create a *potager*-style plot. For a central focal point, a circular pond was an instant talking point amongst a number of old established plot holders. They had never seen the like before and considered it a waste of growing space. As I told Eddie, a retired AA patrolman, 'It will soon attract plenty of frogs and they will eat many slugs.'

He sucked on his pipe and muttered, 'Slug pellets would be a damned sight easier and more effective.'

At the start of the millennium, the majority of allotmenteers on this site were growing using the "kill anything that moves with chemicals" mentality. They applied copious amounts of artificial fertilisers annually. The early years of my allotment coincided with me being instrumental in the development of the organic garden at Newton Rigg. This was my biggest achievement at the college. My colleague Antony Wills said, when I first muted the idea of growing organically, 'What do you know about organic gardening?'

'Not much yet, but I will soon learn,' I replied, without much conviction.

However, both the allotment and the college organic garden produced many excellent crops. On both sites, I introduced a mixture of fruit, vegetables and flowers to attract pollinating insects and useful predators and parasites as a means of pest and disease control. Large compost bays, a wormery and liquid manure-making equipment were added at the college. We introduced organic modules into many courses at Newton Rigg and ran some highly subscribed stand-alone organic courses. My successor Shelagh Todd has doubled the size of the organic garden. It continues to evolve and demonstrate the practice and science of this environmentally and ecologically sound system to Cumbrian students.

I took early retirement from Newton Rigg (which had merged with the University of Central Lancashire in 1998) in 2005. The university was undergoing its third cull of academic staff and offering generous redundancy and retirement packages. My application for early release was accepted. On the 10th of October 2005, I left my office for the final time. I knew I was handing over to the more-than-capable Shelagh. She is one of the best lecturers I worked with in my career. Her empathy with the students meant they reached their maximum potential under her guidance. She is an excellent horticulturalist and garden designer whose enthusiasm has inspired students for decades.

***

1 never missed the routine drudgery of full-time employment. From the very first morning, I felt nothing but relief at not having my mornings dominated by an alarm clock. To know that what I did from then onwards would be what I chose, when I wanted, was a joyous prospect. There would be no more inspections, no more assessments. It felt like the end of a long, harsh winter, with the new buds of spring about to erupt. Eleven years back in Cumbria laid the foundations for the ten happiest years of my career. My time at Newton Rigg had increased my profile to an extent that my services were soon in demand.

***

Writing a weekly gardening column for the *Cumberland News* began in 2003. The college's marketing manager negotiated an agreement with the paper whereby in return for my contribution they would provide free advertising space for our horticultural courses. Following my retirement, my weekly gardening column for the *Cumberland News* continued as before, but with one major difference. The newspaper asked me to continue and paid me. I continued writing regular articles until 2017 when the newspaper became part of "Newsquest", an international organisation whose management decided to discontinue garden features. Other writing projects included a series of articles on gardeners who grew to show for *Cumbria Life* magazine.

In late summer of 2004, I submitted the outline of a proposed book on allotment gardening to the publishers David & Charles. This was at a time when interest and publicity in allotment gardening was beginning to generate interest. The commissioning editor was intrigued by my ideas and we arranged to meet at a hotel on the Cumbrian coast. He was up for the weekend from Cornwall visiting relatives in Cumbria. He bought me lunch as we talked through the book's content and layout. Somewhat surprisingly, he didn't ask to see any evidence of my garden writing. We parted, as I understood it, with a non-written agreement for the book to proceed. Weeks turned into months and I heard nothing from the publishers. Eventually, after constant badgering, I got a reply which bluntly informed me that their marketing department didn't think a book on allotment gardening would sell in sufficient numbers to justify taking the proposal forward. I was deflated and, on reflection, when in the next few years the popularity of allotments really took off, I realised I should have persisted and offered my ideas to more publishers. I was before my time.

***

Being invited to talk to gardening clubs was, for me, more pleasurable than lecturing to groups of students. I enjoyed putting on a performance, and the applause which accompanied the show. My pruning demonstrations were regularly requested. I would arrive at my destination with armfuls of vegetation. This was laid out on tables at the front of the venue. I would make my way from left to right armed with secateurs and loppers. Every sample was picked in turn as I described its main attributes and how and when to prune it.

Spring 2006 saw the first of a number of part-time evening courses which I organised and ran for the Strikes group at their newly opened flagship garden centre at Houghton Hall just outside Carlisle. One day, practical workshops on topics including "The Care of Pot Plants" and "Vegetables in Containers" were added to the offerings as Houghton Hall soon established itself as the primary garden centre in the area. Enrolments on the courses were high, with most participants returning each year.

Teaching practical gardening skills had always been the part of lecturing which I enjoyed the most. I was delighted to be invited to run practical fruit and vegetable growing classes on allotment sites for gardening groups in Carlisle and the nearby village of Wetheral and the small town of Brampton.

The first two years of semi-retirement weren't entirely trouble-free. Bladder problems had been building for a number of years. Toilet visits became more frequent, more urgent and increasingly painful. My doctor organised for me to see a specialist, the upshot of which was a few days in hospital in early November 2006. An operation involved the removal of 200 bladder stones, a sample of which I still possess. They were presented to me in a plastic bottle by the consultant when he saw me a month later for a routine follow-up check.

David in Greenhouse

'These are a few of the offending items which caused the blockage,' he announced as he handed them to me. 'The good news is there was no sign of prostate cancer, so you should be fine in that department for a long time to come. Always drink plenty of water. I don't need to see you again.'

***

In spring 2007, I was invited to act as a Gardens Tours Host by Higham Hall College, an adult residential college based near Bassenthwaite Lake. The job involved taking groups of up to fifteen students on visits to Cumbrian gardens. I would be given accommodation and meals at the college as well as reasonable remuneration. Courses would be three to four days long. The first programme had been planned for me by my predecessor, who had relinquished the role due to pregnancy. It sounded like the ideal job, and that is what it turned out to be.

From the minute I walked into the old hall and into reception, it felt welcoming. The staff were friendly and the atmosphere relaxed. The first course went reasonably well. One difficult person complained about my driving.

I went too fast through a built-up area even though I stayed under the 30 mph limit. She chose a seat over one of the rear wheels and claimed she felt sick. Other group members from the front of the minibus offered to swap seats with her, but she was determined to stay put and moan. Feedback at the end of the course was good enough for me to want to continue. I looked forward to creating any future courses myself. They would be to gardens of my choice. Gardens that I would visit and whose owners/gardeners I would get to know before including them in the itinerary.

Initially, most of the gardens visited were the large ones which opened to the public. These visits included a guided tour by a member of staff (the head gardener where possible). I soon realised that visits to small private gardens were more beneficial. The students could relate to the size of the ground and they enjoyed meeting the owners, who were delighted to show us round and share horticultural tips and stories with fellow gardeners. Wherever we went, we were given tea and coffee to wash down the most delicious assortment of cakes. Some of these gardens featured in the National Gardens Scheme, and the owners were happy to take groups by appointment. Others didn't open their gates to the public, but through my contacts they were happy for me to bring my groups. Such visits became the highlight of my courses.

For the courses to run smoothly, thorough planning was essential. Excellent gardens and friendly, knowledgeable owners were vital. I always checked out new gardens before including them. On many occasions, Barbara accompanied me on this pleasurable chore. As important was selecting suitable locations to eat our packed lunches and the need to programme in toilet stops. Travelling times between gardens were recorded, and gardens in the same part of the county were visited on the same day, thus ensuring the minimum amount of time possible was spent travelling. Seven to ten days before the start of a course, I would contact the garden owners to check that they were expecting us. This meticulous planning paid off on all bar one occasion. On the second of two visits to the same garden, we arrived to find no one at home. My last words on the previous visit had been, 'See you in two weeks' time, Charles, with another group.'

'Look forward to it, David,' was the cheerful reply.

We found a member of staff in a nearby house who phoned Charles' wife, Margaret, who was shopping in Cockermouth. Charles had forgotten and was in a meeting at St Bees. I took the group around the garden and arboretum. Margaret rushed home, and whilst we enjoyed ourselves in the sun, she prepared a fulsome spread of tea and cakes.

The food at Higham Hall was of the highest standard. A bell was rung at mealtimes and the eagerly waiting course members quickly took their places in the dining room. The college provided courses in a wide range of subjects, including art, music, walking and history. Three or four courses would be in residence at the same time. There was a great deal of cross-fertilisation between the various courses. I owe the attention to detail I put into organising the garden tours to the example set by Harry

King at Border Television, who produced the gardening shows in my Newton Rigg days.

In spring of 2011, my garden workload doubled with very little warning. Peter Howarth had amongst his many other horticultural duties, run garden holiday courses for Rothay Manor Hotel in Ambleside. I knew Peter through my involvement on the committee of Cumbria in Bloom. Peter was the chairman. After one meeting, he told me that he was thinking of slowing down a bit.

'I am, after all, nearly eighty. Would you be interested in taking over my Rothay Manor Garden Tours?'

'Yes, I would be happy to when the time comes. That's a long time off yet,' I replied.

'Maybe, but it's good to have you lined up.'

Two weeks later, I got an 8.30 am phone call from Julia, Peter's wife. 'David, it's Julia Howarth. Peter was taken ill in the night. He's not at all well. Can you take over his garden holiday?'

'When?'

'Today if you can.'

'Okay, I can get down for this afternoon. Where are the group meant to be?'

'Visiting Holehird Gardens.'

'All right, I will be there about 2.30 pm. Tell Peter not to worry. I'll look after them until he's back on his feet.'

Although he made a good recovery, Peter was never able to resume his host duties. My stand-in role became permanent.

The hotel courses ran from Sunday evening to Friday morning, with two in spring and one in autumn.

The rate of pay was better than that of Higham Hall, the accommodation superior and food excellent. I preferred the friendlier, more relaxed atmosphere of Higham Hall.

Canapés were served in the hotel bar at 6.15 pm. Afterwards, I gave an illustrated talk before we were called for dinner at 7.30 pm. Coffee and biscuits were then served in the lounge before the guests and I retired to bed at about 10 pm. They were long days. Everyone was grateful for the free Wednesday afternoons built into the holiday. Nonetheless, there was a regular contingency of returners, most of whom booked for next year on the morning of their departure.

Much to my relief, a couple of sisters only came on one gardening holiday. They were always late. Late for breakfast, late getting back on the coach after every garden we visited. They never apologised, either to me or anyone else. This most infuriating habit reached its peak on the occasion when we left the hotel without them. Our transport was about five minutes late when the driver swung into the drive, crunching and splaying the gravel as he skidded to a halt outside the front door.

'Jump in! I'm running a bit late. Got the school run to do before I bring you lot back,' snapped Mr Grumpy.

I always counted people on the coach. But not this time.

When we got to the destination, as usual I counted everyone off.

'Oh no! Where are the sisters?'

No one knew nor cared.

Some ten minutes later, a car pulled up driven by Peter the hotel manager. Out stepped the two sisters. They were adamant that we had left early and they were at the departure point on time. Fortunately, all the other participants took my side and told them in no uncertain terms that they were late as usual. On every succeeding holiday, my regulars never failed to tease me about the day I forgot the sisters.

The hotel used the services of a local bus company for several years. Their vehicles were neither comfortable nor reliable. On a cold, showery May day, we had enjoyed a comforting midday meal in the pub in Mungrisdale when my plans suffered a setback. Kenny, our Liverpudlian driver, put the key into the minibus door. The key stuck; he couldn't turn it or get it out. We were stuck. Or so we thought. To compound the problem, because of the surrounding hills, I couldn't get any reception on my phone to warn the owners of the next garden that we were going to be late. After much persistence with a piece of wire, Kenny managed to get the door window slightly ajar. With great skill, he put a narrow piece of wood (borrowed from the pub) through the window and opened the door latch. We arrived at our next venue only ten minutes late. Kenny had to endure much light-hearted ribbing about his breaking and entering prowess.

***

I was without a dog for almost two years. In April 2006 at the age of fifteen, Nipper had to be put down. Barbara had recently lost her cat Tiddles. Barbara moved in with me in February 2007. We didn't want to remain pet-less any longer. It was time for a new dog. We visited some RSPCA kennels near Gretna. They were looking for homes for a litter of eleven Collie/Staffie pups. All were gorgeous, but one quickly decided she would choose us (she jumped up on my lap and nuzzled into my jumper). It was a mutual attraction. She was too young to leave her mother. We collected her after four weeks and took her home in Tiddles' old cat basket. Peggle (Peg) was so named by us because she was born when the cowslips (commonly called peggles in Essex) were in flower. She was the most amazing dog, being strong, agile, intelligent, very gentle and extremely attractive.

On our daily dog walks in Stanwix and further afield, we swopped dog stories, both happy and sad, with other equally besotted owners. Peg loved her time in the woods. Her favourite walk was in Gelt Woods near the small market town of Brampton. It is a magical site of special sounds. Water in the River Gelt tumbles gently in places and roars in others as it throws stones against the rocks through which it flows. These aquatic sounds are complemented by the plops of jumping trout and melodious birdsong. The effect is like an expertly conducted orchestra. No discord, just perfect harmony and flawless timing. Peg was happy to run, sniff and chase sticks in these woods for hours. Sadly, we lost her aged thirteen after she developed a tumour in her abdomen.

Lizzie our black short-haired cat joined us about a year after Peg. An orphan from the RSPCA, she had a difficult start in life. Being virtually feral, it was years before she became anything approaching domesticated. Since Peg's day, being the only animal in the household, she doesn't have to share our attention. She has thrived in recent months and is much more confident and contented. Her behaviour has become more kittenish with age.

***

February 2007 saw the acquisition of a second allotment. As with the first plot seven years earlier, it needed rabbit-proof fencing erecting around the perimeter. Lots of rotten timber and broken glass were taken in the car to the council recycling centre. This preceded digging and the tedious removal of the roots of couch grass which had been left in a gigantic mound by the previous tenants. A 6 ft by 8 ft greenhouse was a gift from Killer, the plot holder adjacent to our original plot, who was moving to a plot nearer his home. We soon added a second similar-sized greenhouse which we acquired for £30 from another departing tenant. Included in this transaction was an established white grape. Over the years, this provided several litres of delicious grape juice.

We inherited a rickety wooden bench made by the tenant before last. The addition of a few extra nails kept it going until 2015. Frank Philips was a local character whose booming voice could be heard at the far end of the site. An ex-train driver, Frank had at one time been the Liberal candidate for Carlisle. His oratory would certainly

Peggle by Greenhouses 2008

have been received loudly and clearly when he got on his soap box in the centre of town. His biggest claim to vegetable greatness was being the first to plant his seed potatoes. 'They're coming through – look! Seventeenth of March they went in. Earliest of anyone's by far.'

His mate was Willie Bell (teller of the dock story). Both were allotment stalwarts. The opposite of Frank, Willie went about his chores quietly and without bragging. Willie was selective as to when to switch on his hearing aid. Frank would stand near Willie and try to make conversation. 'Can you hear me, Willie?'

'What?'

'Have you got your hearing aid in?'

'Aye.'

'Well, switch it on then.'

A wry smile would break out across Willie's wrinkled face.

Willie saved the seeds of his vegetables and seed potatoes for many years. The sight of his leeks going to seed created a picture that stays fondly in my memories. So does the image of him pedalling home with produce in a box fastened behind the bike seat, and his cross-bred dog Ben on a string lead, running alongside. In Willie's words, he had trained Ben to the bike.

Celia Graham, reverentially known as Mrs Graham, was in her nineties. For decades, she managed two plots and in her younger days held the post of allotment chairman. She cycled across town to her plots every day until a few days before she died aged ninety-four. Her natural inclination to keep order was remembered by all who knew her. She was especially vigilant in her mission to stop the dumping of rubbish on a site near her plots. Sitting in a chair inside her hut, she would harangue anyone passing by pushing a wheelbarrow full of offending goods. 'Where do you think you're going with that? You can't dump it over there.' No one questioned Mrs Graham's authority.

Two allotments meant room to grow a wider range of crops. In fact, far more than we could eat. We bought a freezer which in the autumn was filled with broad beans, peas, tomatoes, raspberries and stewed fruit, including apples and plums. Jams and chutneys were made in large quantities, and a great deal of produce was given to friends and neighbours.

Cooking colourful, healthy food has always been an important part of our relationship. Living together, we soon developed our own efficient system for food preparation. This involves preparing all the ingredients before any cooking takes place. You need an ample area of work surface to do this. To this end, we had the living/dining area converted into a living room and a kitchen/diner. Because we spend so much time cooking and eating, this was the best home improvement we made.

From one or two, we soon acquired dozens of cookery books. Some are still being used regularly with several and in a few cases many recipes being repeated from each book. None have ended up as show books. If we find on the odd occasion one that doesn't appeal, it goes to a charity shop. Over the years, we have learned to tweak recipes to suit our taste buds. This usually involves adding more spice(s) and garlic than indicated. What is the point of one garlic clove? Times stated in cookery books can't always be relied upon. Flexibility in the kitchen is our strategy.

For a couple of years, Barbara and I made curries and sometimes stew for the Carlisle food bank from our surplus vegetables. I couldn't help it; I just loved growing crops. Every year, I would grow something new and was always prepared to keep experimenting with new varieties and new techniques.

The end of 2017 saw us relinquish the most recently acquired plot, including the two greenhouses. We had a super greenhouse at home complete with automatic watering and, with only one plot, it would be easier to go on holidays when we wished.

Back on the original plot, I decided to look afresh at the advantages and disadvantages of digging. Throughout my career, I had always enjoyed great satisfaction when digging. The site of a well-turned plot filled me with pride; the exercise was as good as it gets (no sweaty gym for me). I had, however, seen over the years the excellent results achieved by the advocates of no-dig gardening. So in the autumn of 2018, I took the giant step to experiment by turning half the plot into a trial of the no-dig method.

This reappraisal of such a basic gardening principle resulted from a presentation which Barbara and I attended at Newton Rigg College. It was given by Professor Phil Gregory, an astrophysicist in the Physics and Astronomy Department at the University of British Columbia. He had spent two years investigating the causes of regular soil degradation. Deep cultivation was, along with chemical-intensive farming, deforestation and global warming, proven to be a major contributor.

Fortunately, I had built up a good supply of compost and this was spread to a depth of 7.5 cm on 1.2 metre-wide raised beds ready for spring sowing and planting in 2019. Because of the way events unfolded in the spring, nothing was sown or planted in 2019.

Seventeen

Significant Events of the Last Decade

Our passports were out of date. The last time I had holidayed abroad was 1994 when I took Rachel and Laura to Skiathos. For Barbara, it was a few years prior to that year since she had flown. We had enjoyed several wonderful breaks in Britain and a week in Ireland. Hanging around in airports for hours and the stress of coping with passport control just seemed like too much aggravation.

In June 2011, we took the brave decision to holiday in Tuscany. Check-in at Manchester Airport confirmed our worst fears. After joining a lengthy queue, we approached what I can only describe as an electronic frisking machine. This scanned our bodies and our hand luggage. I came out the other side clean. Barbara didn't. Bleep, bleep, bleep went the infuriating alarm.

'Excuse me, madam, would you step over here,' stated the blank-faced security official.

'Why, what's matter?' asked a worried Barbara.

'We have an activation, madam,' came the stony reply. 'Open your bag onto this tray, please. Scissors are not allowed in hand luggage. Drop them in that bin, please.'

Boarding time was getting near. I was panicking. Then to our great relief, his colleague waved us through.

From Pisa Airport, we hired a car for the week. It was a two-and-a-half-hour drive to the self-catering villa we had rented just outside Montepulciano. Driving on the right-hand side of the road and going through several multi-lane toll booths required both concentration and vigilance. On arrival at our destination, we looked at each other with wide smiles. It was a beautiful villa, surrounded on all sides by a large, immaculately maintained garden. From the patio doors, we overlooked the imposing architecture of Montepulciano on the opposite hillside. The Tuscan countryside was stunning, with rows and rows of vines radiating from the valley bottom like the spokes of a wheel.

I was struck by the growth rate of the plants. A hedge of *Laurus nobilis* (bay) had put on about 45 cm of new foliage already that year (early summer). The front of the villa was shrouded in *Trachleospermum jasminoides* (commonly known as the confederate jasmine or star jasmine). It was smothered in fragrant white flowers. There were never any spent flowers of any plants on the ground when we stepped outside each morning. One morning at daybreak after waking early, Barbara found out why. The gardener

Rachel and Laura in Florence

and his assistant went round early every morning weeding and raking up fallen leaves and petals.

Another morning, I got up early to meet Davos the gardener. There were a few plants I couldn't identify. Maybe he would walk around the garden with me and tell me the names of those with which I was unfamiliar. Neither of us spoke each other's language. This was where the botanical naming of plants aided by a bit of pointing at the specimens I was interested in came to the rescue. Thanks go to Linnaeus, the Swedish botanist, for inventing the binomial system back in the 1700s.

Since that wonderful time, we have enjoyed holidays in La Palma, Madeira, Tuscany again (with my daughters and grandsons), Lake Maggiore, Seville and a very disappointing time in La Gomera (more about that later). Successful holidays in Britain have continued with one ill-fated exception.

***

Mine and Barbara's relationship was solid. We were very happy together. The status quo sailed smoothly on. Other than the occasional minor tiff, there was nothing to rock the steady ship. Life was blissful. Maybe it was because we had both been married before that we didn't dare risk trying it again. What's the point? we thought. If it's not broken, don't fix it. Getting married couldn't possibly improve our situation. It suited us both fine as it was. Let's leave well alone, certainly for now. No need to rush into things. None of that repent at leisure business for us. And so it went on for twenty years.

I didn't plan it. I have never been known for spontaneous actions. This time, I broke from my normal *modus operandi*. It was Saturday, 16th August 2014. Laura and Ben were staying for a couple of days. We were in the Viceroy Indian restaurant, Carlisle, celebrating Barbara's birthday. The waiter took our orders. There and then, without thought or planning, I decided the time was right. I must have looked rather odd. Laura asked me, 'What's the matter, Dad? You all right?'

'Yes I'm fine,'

'You sure?' said Barbara.

At which point, I looked at Barbara and suggested, 'Maybe we should get married. What do you think?'

There was a brief stunned silence before to my relief and joy she replied, 'Why not, that's a great idea.'

'Oh my God, we didn't see that coming,' said Laura.

'You're going to get married before we do,' said Ben, who only earlier that year had asked me permission to marry Laura. It was a request I had been pleased to agree to, albeit one which I thought was no longer commonly asked.

Arrangements were speedily dealt with. We met the registrar on 21st August and booked the ceremony for

Saturday, 18th October 2014 at Tullie House Museum and Art Gallery, Carlisle. The weather was warm; the venue was tastefully decorated. The food was lovely and the whole event went ahead without a hitch. My niece Gail and her husband Julian took great photos, which at a later date they presented to us in an album. It is a great reminder of an extremely happy day.

Our honeymoon was spent in La Gomera (the second smallest of the Canary Islands). It turned out to be our least successful holiday to date. It is a barren, desolate place, with virtually no places of interest to visit. Getting there involved a flight to Teneriffe followed by an hour's ferry journey to the island. After this, it was a scary taxi journey of another hour and a half to our accommodation. Roads without crash barriers snaked up and down the mountainous terrain, hairpin bends being a regular feature. Our driver spent a lot of time with one hand on the steering wheel whilst he texted with the other. His eyes alternated between his phone and the road. The apartment didn't live up to the description on the website. The photographs on the website were, we decided, taken several years ago. This dissatisfaction was compounded by the exceptionally hot weather. It was too hot to move, even to sleep. This was caused by unexpected hot winds blowing in from Africa. Even the locals found it unbearable.

Despite this disastrous trip, we were delighted to be married. Why didn't we do it before? I don't know. That doesn't matter; we were happy before and we are happy now – possibly even happier now.

***

In October 2015, ten years after retiring from full-time employment, I decided to call a halt to most of my part-time paid activities. I wanted to stop when I knew I was still capable of doing a really good job. After a few months of mental inertia, I was aching for a new stimulus. A writing course had its appeal. Maybe with guidance and encouragement I could write my memoirs.

After seeing a flyer in The Kirkby Stephen Bookshop, I discovered the impetus I needed. Vicki Bertram was planning to run a writing workshop from her home in the fells above Kirkby Stephen. The upshot was that Barbara and I joined the inaugural meeting on 3rd November 2016. We signed up for several series of workshops over the next three years. Vicki cajoled, praised and helped everyone in the group to strive to reach their limits, setting us new challenges after every workshop. Members of the group were very supportive of each other, offering positive feedback on our writing, which we read at every meeting.

From Carlisle, it took us just over an hour to Kirkby Stephen. We travelled by far the furthest. But the venue was an added bonus. The regular trips to the area where I grew up provided umpteen jolts to kick-start many reminiscences of my formative years. So why did we stop attending Vicki's workshops? Well, that simply boils down to distance. A journey of fifty miles each way was doable. However, another unexpected development meant that twice as far wasn't feasible.

***

It was twenty-five years since I had lived in the Cambridgeshire village of Papworth Everard. My old house was in close proximity to Papworth Hospital. The hospital wasn't visible from my house or the road which passed through the village. I was told back in 1993 that it began life as a tuberculosis colony and was now renowned for heart, liver and lung transplants. I lived at 13 Dengaine Close for less than a year. Moving back to Cumbria wasn't part of my plans when I bought the house. Moving back to Papworth certainly wasn't planned.

In early July, 2018, a holiday brought Barbara and I back to East Anglia. We rented a cottage in Swaffam, Norfolk. After two days, at Barbara's insistence, we visited the local health surgery. I explained to the nurse/practitioner that I had felt discomfort in my chest. After a few tests, including blood pressure and heart rate, she summoned an ambulance. Within twenty minutes, I was on my way to the Queen Elizabeth Hospital, King's Lynn. Barbara came with me.

Within minutes, I had electrodes stuck on my chest and arms. This, I was told by Elliot, the younger of the two paramedics, was an ECG. His slightly older supervisor watched the readings on a monitor. He then drew me a diagram of what the pattern should look like on the condensation of the ambulance window. My graph went up where it should have gone down. (Or was it the other way round?) Anyway, it showed something was amiss. The paramedics were very composed and kept me calm. So I assumed there wasn't much wrong with me.

At the hospital, I was put in a monitoring and assessment ward for twenty-four hours before being transferred to a cardiac ward. A senior nurse visited me, and when she asked how I was feeling, I cheerily said, 'I feel fine. In fact, I feel a bit like a fraud being in here.'

'Oh no, you're not a fraud. You've had a heart attack. Tomorrow you will be taken by ambulance to Papworth, where they will fit a stent.'

'But we are on holiday and have to leave the cottage we are renting on Saturday, and I have to drive home to Cumbria.'

'Well, that's not going to happen. If you don't have this done, the next heart attack might be your last, Mr Haigh.'

On the journey to Papworth, I was bombarded by a very verbose, well-intentioned paramedic. For ninety minutes, I was privy to his career history in the NHS, most of which had been spent at Papworth. He now worked for a private company and I was being transported in one of their ambulances.

It was, he told me, 'an excellent company who employ fully trained paramedics and fit out their ambulances with the full range of equipment. Lots of private firms operate with the only minimum investment in both staff and essential equipment.'

His affection for Papworth was deep and genuine. It wouldn't be the same when the hospital moved to a new home towards the end of 2018. Staff, he told me, were already leaving rather than having to travel the twenty miles to Cambridge where they would have to pay astronomical car parking charges.

'But don't worry, they will soon sort you out. Best hospital in the world for heart problems. Just turning into the main drive now.'

'Already? Gosh, that went really quickly!' I said, trying to sound genuine.

I was taken to a bay with five other chatty old boys. Introductions over and in came a couple of doctors. They headed for my bed.

The senior doctor asked how long it was since I stopped smoking. He seemed quite happy with my fourteen years ago answer.

His next question, which related to alcohol, drew a very different response. 'How many units a week do you have?'

No point lying, I thought, so I blurted out, 'Seventy.'

'Seven,' he responded.

'No, seventy a week,' I repeated.

His genuine look of horror and sadness was a vision I will always remember.

'Apart from any damage to your heart, if you carry on drinking at that rate, you will ruin your liver.'

I haven't touched a drop of alcohol since.

I was given a brief explanation of what they would do with me at 2.30 pm provided no emergency admissions caused a delay.

It sounded like a simple, straightforward task. In fact, I was somewhat disappointed when they referred to it as a procedure. It didn't sound anything like as major as the operation I was expecting. Reality hit home when the consultant told me the odds of something going wrong were 1000 to 1. I said nothing, but inwardly this didn't seem a very good bet. Still, better than doing nothing, I reasoned.

My spirits rose even higher when I realised I was the oldest of the six and I only needed one stent. The others had more complex heart problems than me.

Before long, Barbara arrived with my two very worried-looking daughters. Rachel had phoned me, not knowing what had happened, when I was in King's Lynn Hospital. Laura drove her and her elder sister down from Derbyshire that morning. They had picked Barbara up on the way. It wasn't visiting hours, but the staff nurse allowed them to stay for twenty minutes.

With 2.30 pm approaching, I was taken to the procedure room. Barbara, Rachel and Laura were in close attendance. The confidence of the staff put me at ease. Yes, it was routine for them, but their relaxed yet professional demeanour dissipated all my anxiety. They told me I could watch every stage on a nearby screen. I declined this offer. As they got to work, my thoughts went to all the groundbreaking heart surgery without which me and thousands more would have had their lives considerably curtailed. I recalled first hearing the news of the world's first heart transplant. I was twenty years old. The year was 1967. The operation was performed by Dr Christiaan Barnard in Cape Town, South Africa. In 1979, Britain's first successful heart transplant was carried out at Papworth by Sir Terence English. 1986 saw Papworth conduct the world's first heart, lung and liver transplant. I mused that the famous surgeons who carried out these and many other operations must have performed in this very room. To refer to them as the celebrities of their profession would now seem in the light of the current interpretation of celebrity to belittle their achievements. They will, however, be revered for much longer than the likes of most of the contestants on inaccurately, so-called talent shows, who enjoy somewhat fleeting adoration.

Only thirty-five minutes later, I was being unplugged and taken back to the ward. My thanks to the staff were inadequate.

The following morning, two senior doctors did their rounds and told me I was being released later that day. Barbara and Rachel collected me and we all spent our last night in the cottage in Swaffham.

Next day, Rachel drove us back home to Carlisle.

***

'David, it's the removal men,' called Barbara.

'Okay, coming! It's only eight o'clock. They weren't supposed to arrive until nine thirty.' As I came down the stairs, I was greeted by a tall, slim forty-something-year-old with a craggy face.

'Morning, boss. I'm Keith.'

'You're very early. We were told it would be nine thirty to ten.'

'Aye, well, plans change,' came the cheery response in a broad north eastern accent. 'We've got to travel down to

Aylesbury for the next job later today. Just seeing where I can park the truck,' said Keith, pointing down the street to where the giant vehicle stood. 'It'll go over there, that's fine.'

I showed him what had to go. Nothing fazed him until we came to the dismantled greenhouse. A worried frown creased his forehead.

'The guy who did the quotation said it was no problem to transport.'

'Well, he doesn't have to do it, does he? Just presses buttons on his tablet. That's hardest work he ever does.'

'Oh! You will stack the glass carefully, won't you? It costs £40 a sheet.'

'How about a coffee then, before we start? If you don't ask, you don't get. I'll call the lad from the lorry. Milk and two sugars in both, please.'

By noon, the lorry was loaded. Our car was bursting at the seams. We wanted to reach our destination first as we had to collect the keys to our new home by 2 pm. The couple we bought the house from reckoned they would have left by 12.30 pm. Unfortunately, their removal firm had miscalculated the amount to be moved and sent too small a lorry. When we arrived, men were standing around waiting for a second lorry to arrive to take all the things from the shed, garage and garden. When it drew up, our two men, who had been brilliant throughout, helped to load up, much to the relief of the stressed Wilma (by now previous owner) and her sister.

Keith and his nameless mate gave various rooms names. All the paintings and Barbara's artists' equipment went in the art room. Dozens of boxes of books ended up in the library and according to Keith I had gone up in the world because I now had an office. By 5.30 pm, all our belongings were somewhere in the house or garage. Nothing was broken; nothing was damaged. Despite the less-than-optimistic weather forecast, it didn't rain. After such an achievement, our thoughts turned to alcohol. It was incidentally a year to the day since the demon drink had passed our lips. But we didn't succumb.

Moving to Scotland was never considered before March 2019. Barbara and I had visited Dumfries and Galloway several times over the last twelve years or so. Notions of living in a different place kept erupting like a rash. But always to somewhere in England. We'd even looked at houses in Ripon and the Belper area of Derbyshire. Each time, we had returned home disappointed. The houses weren't right for us. Wherever we chose was too noisy and too busy. Staying in Carlisle seemed by far the best option.

When the itch flared up again in spring 2019, we decided to see what south west Scotland had to offer. A few internet searches led to the bookmarking of a few properties in our price range. Encouragingly, it seemed you got more house for your money in desirable areas than you did in Cumbria. We saved a number of houses worth viewing in case we decided to pursue the idea of emigrating. On 13th March, we flew from Edinburgh to Seville for a week's holiday. House hunting thoughts were shelved for the duration. They resurfaced soon after our return.

On Saturday 30th March, we arranged to view two properties in Castle Douglas. We were impressed by the size, presentation and location of the first house. The second one was a disappointment. It was over-priced and very badly presented. Two weeks later, we returned to 8 Longacre Road for a second viewing and to check a few measurements. The house was as good as our first sightings had indicated. Not wanting to rush into a decision without some further thought, and seeing one more property, we, along with Peg (our thirteen-year-old Collie/Staffie cross), stayed the night in Castle Douglas at the Ernespie Hotel. Next day, we went back to No 8, chatted some more to Graham and Wilma, the sellers, and verbally agreed a price for what was to become our new home.

We employed a solicitor who was registered with the Scottish Law Society. The process of buying the house went through swiftly and smoothly. We moved in on Friday,

Barbara in Galloway

7th June 2019. Much to our relief, we had an offer which we accepted for our house in Carlisle three days before moving. The sale of the house in Carlisle completed on 9th Sept 2019. We feel very fortunate to own such a spacious house on a small residential development on the edge of town. Castle Douglas has everything we need, including a range of small privately owned shops, two supermarkets, a library, dentist's, a medical centre and a frequent bus service.

To date, we have driven through lots of attractive countryside and visited the artists' town of Kirkcudbright several times and Scotland's largest book town of Wigtown. Many visits have so far been enjoyed to the wonderful Threave Garden, situated in the parish of Castle Douglas and owned by the National Trust for Scotland.

***

The biggest gardening success to date has been the dismantling, removal and re-erection of the greenhouse. The tomato plants, chilli peppers and cucumber plant which started life in the greenhouse in Carlisle travelled to Castle Douglas in the car and had to survive outdoors for two weeks until the greenhouse went up in its new home. All the plants romped away in their new abode. The tomato plants each produced five trusses of fruit. The sole cucumber plant produced twelve fruits.

It only took a few months to get our new home in Castle Douglas sorted to our liking. We loved it when we moved in and still do. It is the first house we have chosen and bought together. It is our home. Barbara's influence is evident in every room by her choice of absorbing pictures. Room for more bookcases amply demonstrates her lifelong love of reading. Conversion of a large part of the garage to a studio for Barbara to pursue various art projects is underway.

By the end of summer, I could wait no longer. The ground outside had to be tackled. It had been left neat and tidy. Low-maintenance and sterile, it was laid mainly to grass, concrete kerb edgings and concrete paving. But it was not a garden. All the kerbs and at least half of the paving would have to go.

So out came the pick, sledgehammer, fork and spade. Behaving like a forty-year-old, I began prising up the kerbs. With a worried frown, Barbara approached from the kitchen. 'Are you sure you should be doing that? It looks really hard work. I think you should hire someone to do that kind of thing!'

'Oh, it's fine! I've done this sort of thing before. Plenty of times.'

'You were much younger then, AND you hadn't had a heart attack.'

Stubbornly, I kept on. Next morning, as I got out of bed, my left ankle made me acutely aware of the folly of my actions. It was red, swollen and too painful to put pressure on. Two weeks later, with my ankle back to normal, I resumed excavations. Within days, my back was causing enough pain to make finding a comfortable sleeping position difficult. I conceded to Barbara's wise words and called in the cavalry. David Lewis and his son Joe spent three days lifting the remaining concrete and taking at least five trailer loads of this and other rubbish to the tip. Their biggest challenge was the destruction with a pneumatic drill of an extremely ugly and exceedingly heavy granite bridge. As David said whilst wiping the sweat which ran in rivulets down his face, 'Everything about this place is heavy duty.'

Next up was the "big dig". The solid compacted ground meant no option but to dig. The soil structure had been seriously damaged by builders' machinery. Both front and back gardens had to have the severely compacted soil broken up. The front garden slopes away from the house and was better drained than the back. It's also much smaller, so to gain some early incentive it was the first to receive the deep fork treatment. The grass was buried upside down and chopped up under each trench, thereby retaining valuable organic matter. Planting with trees, shrubs, perennials, biennials and spring flowering bulbs was completed in November.

When the rains abated, the back garden was tackled. It was a much larger, more strenuous undertaking. The soil is very heavy clay. This is as a result of the builders terracing the land at the rear of the gardens with their earth-moving machinery. The two terraces above the houses were planted with a variety of trees, including alder, larch, beech and oak in order to stabilise the terraces and absorb excess water. This landscaping has been very successful, and the residents now benefit from the aesthetic and functional features of trees and the developing habitat provided for wildlife. The birdsong is a delight. We are frequently entertained by the gliding, effortless flight of red kites.

These majestic birds of prey have been successfully reintroduced into Galloway by the RSPB.

The downside has been the moving of top soil up the hill, which has exposed mostly clay subsoil at the bottom where the gardens are situated. My solution after the initial deep cultivation to break up the hard layers is to treat the soil with gypsum and dried seaweed meal. These natural substances will improve over time the aeration and drainage by binding the clay particles (known as flocculation) together without changing the pH. In addition, I will add copious quantities of organic matter in the form of garden compost, farmyard manure and seaweed products.

Plans for a *potager*-style back garden are evolving. Fruit trees, including apple, plum, cherry and, at Barbara's request, fig, will give height to the layout and form a link to the adjoining block of trees. Strawberries, redcurrants, blackcurrants and blueberries will form the lower connecting layer from trees to vegetables and herbs. Flowers chosen for their attraction to pollinating insects will be sown in abundance. Oh, and I couldn't create a garden without a pond. This will be sited near the arbour which came from the Carlisle garden. The creation of a new garden is just so wonderful. The inevitable plant failures or plant combinations which don't work all add to further opportunities to try different plants in different places. Fortunately, no one has yet nor ever will create the perfect garden.

Other than minimal soil disturbance in subsequent years, I don't anticipate any major digging.

The benefits to soil health through no-dig gardening are so convincing. They may be summarised thus:

- digging releases carbon dioxide into the atmosphere, thereby contributing to global warming
- deep cultivation destroys the structure built by bacteria and fungi, turning the soil into sterile land
- when undisturbed, bacteria and fungi build underground cities for microbes to live in, with channels for air and water to penetrate to greater depths
- microbes are responsible for healthy soil, creating biotic glues and fungal strands which bind the soil together
- digging brings weed seeds to the surface where they readily germinate to produce further generations
- earthworms and other beneficial creatures are at the mercy of predators after being exposed on the surface by digging

The reasons for digging and how to dig correctly were instilled in me at the start of my career. Digging tests were an integral part of all horticultural qualifications. I always took great pride in the end product. Over fifty-seven years, I have dug many acres of soil, often digging the same patch several times over the years. In my career, I taught hundreds of students how to dig. So even though I have enjoyed digging all my life and always considered it an essential element of my gardening life, then maybe, just maybe, I will dig no more.

***

Even without digging, plenty of hard graft lay ahead. I opted for a formal layout of straight paths and rectangular beds. The position and width of the paths was marked out with string lines. Six months of endless rain meant walking on the soil was impossible. Boots sunk and stuck in the glue-like earth. Waiting for dry weather tested my patience to the extreme. The excessive rain was, however, the deciding factor in my choice of path material.

Having got rid of dozens of concrete paving slabs, I certainly wasn't buying any more. Grass paths were considered, but only briefly. They would soon wear down to mud. So I opted for bark. Laying perforated plastic below the bark is often recommended as a means of stopping weed growth. But I ignored this much-touted advice. The use of plastic in the garden is to be avoided. It will remain in the soil indefinitely. The edges fray and tiny pieces get ingested by wildlife. I didn't want anything to impede water flow down into the soil. I also wanted worms and other beneficial soil fauna to pull the decaying bark into the ground, thereby improving its structure. In any case, what's wrong with a few weeds? (Fifty years ago, I never thought I would say that.) By spreading a metre-long length with bark to a depth of 50 mm in front of me, I was able to stand on this before spreading the next metre. When completed, we could get around the garden without causing soil compaction.

The problem with a bark path is the speed with which it breaks down. In addition, its dark colour didn't contrast sufficiently with the soil. Hardwood chips were the answer. They are lighter in colour (buff) and much harder wearing. I had used them in my previous garden and on the allotment, so we knew they would be ideal. A 25 mm layer on top of the bark did the trick. Fortunately, we were able to collect bags of these chips in the car a few weeks prior to lockdown.

The advent of lockdown coincided with a complete contrast in the weather. We had no meaningful rain from early March to early June. Garden construction is now complete. The bare bones of the skeleton are in place. This creative and physical phase has been a gratifying diversion from the all-enveloping ramifications of Covid-19.

Two timber raised beds and a pond were ordered from a firm north of Inverness. WoodblocX service and its products proved to be excellent. The blocks of timber fitted together with ease. A third raised bed along the side of the house was made from pressure treated timber obtained from builders' merchants.

Good-quality top soil was bought to fill all the raised beds and to top up the garden soil to a depth of 50 mm. Eight big (1,000-litre) bags in total.

Closure of the local recycling centre meant nowhere to dispose of the bags or the pallets on which they were delivered. The builders' merchant stopped delivering materials a few days before they were due to bring me timber. I could wait until restrictions were lifted or have a refund.

I had decided that the garden paths lacked definition, on top of which birds were scratching and spreading the wood chip surface.

Knowing it would involve a lot of hard work, I decided to dismantle the pallets and edge the paths with the planks. After all, I would have ample time and it would get me fit and keep boredom at bay. Barbara, a firm disciple of recycling and reusing, was delighted at my suggestion. After several days of heavy hammering with a lump hammer and cold chisel, the pallets had yielded enough lengths of useful timber. More than enough for edging the beds and for making supporting pegs.

Barbara bought dark green paint online which matched the greenhouse perfectly. The end result was darned near perfect. Not only was it very satisfying to achieve such an outcome, but it resulted in a refund of approximately £160. This money was soon gobbled up by seeds and plants. With garden centres closed, I had to buy these on the internet.

Buying plants online just doesn't compare to visiting a reputable local nursery or garden centre. Picking out plants and checking for strong healthy growth, good (but not pot-bound) root systems and well-balanced specimens is such a pleasurable part of the buying experience. Alas, during lockdown, that was not to be. To be fair – the quality of the aquatic plants bought for initially stocking the pond was impressive; they arrived in good health and soon got established.

Vegetables including broad beans, runner beans, courgettes, turnips and beetroot have joined the fruit (apple, plum, cherry, blackcurrants, strawberries and fig) which were planted before the pandemic. Seeds of annual flower meadows, dahlia tubers and gladioli corms have been sown/planted to fill in the spaces and tumble over the straight edges of the square/rectangular beds. The aim is to create a colourful *potager*-style effect in this first year. This combination of formal design and the softening effect of informal planting will be added to with more plants, especially wall shrubs and climbers when restrictions are lifted.

Every spring, the resurgence of plants and the renewal of all life is a joyous time. This year has, more than any other, made me appreciate how wonderful my life in gardening has been and continues to be.